CHEVROLET PICKUP
COLOR HISTORY

Tom Brownell and Mike Mueller

Motorbooks International
Publishers & Wholesalers

*I dedicate this book to the memory of
Irv Neubert and Grover Swank,
two old truck friends who are greatly missed*

First published in 1994 by Motorbooks International Publishers & Wholesalers, PO Box 2, 729 Prospect Avenue, Osceola, WI 54020 USA

Motorbooks International books are also available at discounts in bulk quantity for industrial or sales-promotional use. For details write to Special Sales Manager at the Publisher's address

Library of Congress Cataloging-in-Publication Data
Brownell, Tom.
   Chevrolet pickup color history/Tom Brownell, Mike Mueller.
      p. cm.
   Includes index.
   ISBN 0-87938-876-5
   1. Chevrolet trucks—History. 2. Chevrolet trucks—Collectors and collecting. 3. Chevrolet trucks—Pictorial works. I. Mueller, Mike. II. Title.
TL230.5.C45B757   1994
629.223—dc200 94-1461

Printed and bound in Hong Kong

On the front cover: From the Advance Design series, a 1950 model 3100, owned by Ray Morrison, Apopka, Florida

On the frontis page: The elegant hood ornament of a 1935 Suburban owned by Walter Deck, Ridge Farm, Illinois.

On the title page: A smart-looking 1957 3100 pickup, owned by Bob and Debbie Higgins, Davie, Florida.

On the back cover: Ready for farm work is a 1956 Cameo owned by Bob and Linda Ogle, Champaign, Illinois;1993 K3500 extended cab 4X4 dooley. *Chevrolet Motor Division*

Contents

Acknowledgments

I wish to thank my many friends, particularly the members of the Light Commercial Vehicle Association (LCVA), who have helped with research and photos for this book. Also appreciated are the interest and research assistance of Jim Benjaminson, who provided valuable information for the history of 1930-33 Chevrolets; Denny Albertson, who informed me about the limited production S-10 Cameo pickup; and Ric Hall, who sent photos and information on his infectiously cute "shorty snub-nosed" cab-over-engine pickup.

A unique truck for vendors of various products such as fresh produce was the Canopy Express. A 1946 model is shown here. Its owner is Walter Deck, Ridge Farm, Illinois.

Introduction and Trends

**Chevrolet Light-duty Trucks:
The Collector's Favorite**

The Heartbeat of America... With that slogan, Chevrolet has captured what its trucks have meant to new-truck owners and vintage-truck collectors alike. Why the heartbeat, that critical, life-giving energy? Quite simply, during most years, from their start in 1918 to the present day, 1994, Chevrolet models have been the light-truck sales leaders. More Chevrolet trucks are working on farms and traveling the highways than are trucks of any other make. That means if you pull up to your driveway with a Chevy Advance Design pickup in tow—your latest, or first, restoration project—your neighbor isn't likely to say just, "Hey, isn't that a 1953 Chevrolet?" Instead, he'll probably come over to inspect your new purchase more closely and comment, "You know, my Uncle George had a truck just like that; I remember riding in it on his farm," or, "My high school friend Bill drove a truck like that; we sure had good times in it." It's memories like these that make Chevy trucks America's "heartbeat."

There's not a Chevy truck I don't like. Any year or model would be welcome in my garage. And that's how this book looks at the gamut of light trucks General Motors (GM) has built over the last three-quarters of a century... and counting. But, as with any jewels, some have more value potential than others. So, for those who

may be interested in combining ownership of a collector truck with maybe a little equity building, here's a glimpse into this Chevy truck fancier's crystal ball.

Trends and Predictions

Predicting which models of Chevy light trucks will increase most in value during the coming years really has nothing to do with psychic phenomena. Several things in play today give a quite reliable indication of where collector interest will be tomorrow. These predictors include parts support, media attention, and current trends in collector interest and value patterns. Matching these indicators to various Chevrolet truck models clearly shows two styling series leading the pack. These are Chevy's 1947–55 Advance Design models, and Chevrolet pickups and Blazers from the 1969–72 Integrated Styling series.

One reason collectors have made Chevy's Advance Design pickups their number one favorite is simply that so many of these trucks exist. Chevrolet built this styling series for eight-and-a-half years and topped the sales charts the entire period. But I'm sure Advance Design trucks are popular for another, more subtle reason: they seem to be practically everyone's idea of an old truck. Here, too, we're talking about numbers. Most of today's old-car and -truck collectors grew up during the time when Chevy's Advance Design

trucks were doing their yeoman's duty—working in practically every imaginable setting from farms to filling stations. So when someone says, "I just bought an old truck," it's natural for our mind's eye to "see" an Advance Design Chevy.

The 1969-72 Integrated Styling models are popular for a different reason. These were GM's first truly modern trucks, which means they ride almost as smoothly as cars and can be equipped with most car comforts as well. The Integrated Styling models also had an extremely attractive design that has aged like good wine. These trucks look as good today as they did when they were introduced in the turbulent days of the late sixties.

Purchase either an Advance Design or Integrated Styling model Chevy truck, and you will have a collector vehicle that will draw lots of admiring glances and should appreciate faster than money in the bank.

Advance Design Series: Chevrolet's "Classic" Pickup, 1947-1955

The styling features of the Advance Design series, most notably the high-rounded nose and tall windshield, give these trucks a classic pickup look. Let your mind roll back to the days of your youth, picture the trucks you saw parked at the feed store or in front of the hardware, and most likely you're seeing Advance Design Chevys. The Advance Design series was the first example of truck styling getting a

Chevy trucks of the 1967-72 styling series are quickly becoming collector favorites—as seen by the numbers of these trucks that are displayed at shows, the growing parts availability, and rising prices. Reasons for their popularity include outstanding styling and the availability of modern comfort conveniences such as power steering and brakes, automatic transmission, even factory-installed air conditioning. The example shown here is a 1968 Custom model owned by J. R. Meadows of Stanardsville, Virginia.

jump on cars: although Chevrolet's all-new postwar trucks appeared in 1947, the restyled car line didn't make its debut until 1949.

All Chevy Advance Design trucks could be special ordered with the deluxe five-window cabs. Standard cabs had three windows—two in the doors and one in the back. The deluxe cab added curved corner windows that give nearly panoramic visibility and intensified these trucks' already handsome looks. Although strikingly different in appearance from its predecessors, the Advance Design series continued Chevy's familiar light-truck models. Starting with the popular pickup, the Advance Design light-duty line-up included a

panel delivery, the canopy express, a cab-chassis (this was a pickup without the box, originally purchased for use as a wrecker, fire truck, service truck, telephone truck, or some other special use), a people-hauling Carryall Suburban, and a very rare Cantrell-bodied woodie wagon. Although Chevrolet did not build four-wheel-drive pickups until the sixties, toward the end of the Advance Design series, Chevy dealers sold four-wheel-drive conversions for pickups and Suburbans. Today, trucks with this aftermarket all-wheel-drive option are extremely rare and desirable.

Collector preferences among the Advance Design series are short-box half-ton pickups with the deluxe cab, chrome bumpers, and chrome grillework (where authentic), with accessories like a radio and a side-mounted spare. Pickup buyers had a limited choice of dress-up items, but period accessories such as spotlights and sun visors were available, and these are also popular with collectors. Needless to say, any Advance Design pickup with the Napco Mountain Goat four-wheel-drive conversion is a collector prize.

1969–1972 Integrated Styling Series: Another Collector Favorite

The Integrated Styling series actually began in 1967, but the first two years don't command quite as strong a collector following as the others. This series marks Chevy's first truly modern trucks. Equipped with independent front suspension (also available on the Advance Design series), deluxe interiors, air conditioning, power steering, power brakes, predominantly V-8 engines, and automatic transmissions, Chevy and GMC trucks from this series are both comfortable to ride in and easy to drive. In addition, they are extremely good-looking.

Although a large share of Chevy trucks in this series are still working—and sell for the price of used trucks—well-preserved examples command handsome prices and are in strong demand. Don't be surprised to see exceptionally clean lower-production models such as the Longhorn camper specials or the Cheyenne—which were factory equipped with options, such as air conditioning and the toolbox that mounted in the side of the box—selling in the five-figure price range in the very near future. Good-looking and practical, the Integrated Styling Chevy trucks had only one negative feature: poor fuel economy when V-8 powered.

Value Plus

Nearly all Chevrolet light trucks are value leaders, so it's hard to go wrong when picking a truck with the bow-tie (or GMC) emblem. Still, the best advice to would-be collectors is: Don't buy a car, a truck, or any other collectible item just because someone—even me—predicts a rise

in value. Buy what *you* like. That way, you'll have a purchase you can enjoy. If it proves to be a sound investment—which a vintage Chevrolet truck should be—then you have the best of both worlds.

Owners and admirers of GMC trucks should realize that everything said in this book about Chevrolet trucks applies to their trucks, too. From the mid-thirties on, Chevrolet and GMC have been first cousins in the "kissin' cousins" sense. They have shared the same sheet metal and similar engineering, with GMC having the advantage in more powerful and more rugged engines and a correspondingly aggressive image established by the bold, forceful grille—first introduced with GMC's own Advance Design models. In recent years, since 1967 at least, Chevrolet and GMC trucks more closely resemble identical twins distinguished by a crew cut or a moustache. They're really the same truck, differently badged. Some collectors gravitate to trucks with the GMC nameplate because of familiarity, others because GMC's lower production makes these trucks rarer

The most enjoyable part of owning an older truck is joining a club and participating in its activities. This line-up of fifties-vintage Chevrolet trucks was assembled as part of a gathering sponsored by the Northeast Chevy/GMC Club.

and thus less seldom seen. So whether your brand loyalty is Chevrolet or GMC is really just a matter of personal preference.

Since this book has been written with collectors in mind, you may wonder why its coverage extends to the present day. The answer is simple: Chevrolet is still building collector trucks. There is little question in my mind that some of today's Chevy pickups—perhaps the limited production SS 454 or the classic stepside—will undoubtedly be popular with tomorrow's collectors. Chevy didn't build losers. All the trucks in this seventy-eight-year parade have their special appeal. If you're not already a Chevy truck owner, don't let this book be a substitute for the real thing. Find the Chevy truck that matches your interests, and join the fun.

Chapter 1

Beginnings, 1918-1930

Chevrolet entered the light-truck market in 1918 with two models. One was a 490 passenger car chassis fitted only with front fenders, a hood, and a cowl and marketed as a half-ton truck (to which buyers installed a body built by some other manufacturer). The other was a new one-ton cab-chassis fitted with the engine and transmission from Chevrolet's FA series cars. As might be expected, Chevrolet called the half-ton model the 490 Commercial, but, incomprehensible as it may seem, the one-ton truck was dubbed the Model T. How did Chevrolet have the nerve to call its new truck a Model T, a direct copy of its arch competitor's name? Surely it was no secret that Ford had used the name Model T on millions of cars and pickups built since 1909. Apparently manufacturers thought less of their trade

Although America is now described as having a largely service economy, in the earlier part of this century businesses provided their customers with many more services than is the case today. One of the services expected from businesses was home delivery. For this reason, delivery trucks were among the best-selling light-duty models. The Chevrolet delivery truck seen here is a 1928 model, recognized by a taller radiator than earlier models. This was the last year for Chevrolet's four-cylinder engine. This vehicle is owned by Ivan and Verna Birkey of Rantoul, Illinois. Its body was built by Colling Carriage Company, which had outlets in Philadelphia, Camden, and Baltimore.

Flowing fender lines and sporty wire wheels marked Chevrolet's 1930 car models and the roadster pickup as well.

names in those early years of the automobile industry, because Chevrolet continued to call its one-ton trucks Model Ts through 1922.

Unlike Ford, which built its trucks complete and ready-to-work, Chevrolet supplied only the chassis and forward sheet metal, and left the selection of the body to the buyer. This approach offered some advantages. Buyers could move a body off their old truck and put it on their new Chevrolet chassis, or they could select the style of body they wanted—instead of taking what came off the assembly line at the factory. Express or delivery wagons and depot hacks were the most popular body styles. The Martin Perry Company of Indianapolis built most of the bodies used on early Chevrolet trucks, though Hercules and Superior bodies were also popular. Some buyers had the body on their new truck custom built by a local cabinetmaker. The point is, an early Chevrolet truck could have been fitted with almost any imaginable type of cargo body.

The 490 Commercial chassis had a greater load-carrying capacity than the car chassis by virtue of heavier springs. The truck also differed from a 1918 Chevrolet car because the cowl and open-car windshield came from a 1916 model. Besides the cowl and windshield, buyers of the one-ton Model T also got a seat, but no cab. To give the Chevrolet Model T truck enough pulling power for truck-sized

In building its early trucks, Chevrolet supplied only the chassis and forward sheet metal, to which bodies by outside manufacturers were added, by either the buyer or the Chevrolet dealer. This 1926 X series Chevrolet undergoing restoration by Winross Restorations in Palmyra, New York, is a very good representation of what a Chevrolet truck would have looked like when it left the factory. To complete the truck, the talented staff at Winross built a wooden delivery-style body. The finished truck has won many honors, including the prestigious Antique Automobile Club of America Senior Award.

work, a low-reduction worm drive differential replaced the car's ring-and-pinion rear end. Given the metallurgy of the time, worm drive also proved more durable in pulling heavy loads. But the lower gearing also carried the penalty of slower road speeds. However, speed trucks had not yet appeared and no one expected a truck to go fast. Chevrolet continued the pattern of basing its light-duty trucks on a passenger car chassis and using a car engine into the thirties.

Early Chevrolet trucks are extremely rare. Production for that first year totaled only 879—and that number included both models. Truck sales for 1919 rose substantially, to 8,000, which was the total production of half- and one-ton models. But these were still very small numbers compared with those of Ford, which was turning out light trucks by the tens of thousands. Owing to the short but severe post–World War I recession, Chevrolet made few changes to help improve sales. In 1921, arrangements were made with several body suppliers to deliver light-truck bodies directly to Chevrolet assembly plants. This gave buyers the option of purchasing trucks with bodies already mounted. The body options for the 490 Commercial included an open express; a covered express, called a farm wagon; a body nearly identical to the farm wagon, but with seats, called a station wagon; and an enclosed delivery wagon. The Model T one-ton could be fitted with similar bodies, though larger in scale. Chevrolet's 1921 truck brochure also showed the 1921 Model T fitted out as a bus as well as a fire truck with all the hoses and ladders.

Early Chevrolet trucks were also outfitted as fire engines. Surviving examples are extremely rare, but even more remarkable is the fact that the owner of this LM series has been able to locate all the correct fire truck accessories.

That year, Chevrolet also introduced an intermediate-sized three-quarter-ton truck called the Model G, which used the same engine and forward sheet metal as the 490 Commercial but had a longer, 120-inch (in) wheelbase. The longer wheelbase gave the Model G significantly more cargo capacity than the short, 102in-wheelbase model 490 Commercial.

The 490 Commercial and Chevrolet's one-ton Model T were built through 1922. Changes were insignificant with the exception that pneumatic tires replaced solid rubber on the one-ton Model T at some point in its four-year production run. When the 490 Commercial's replacement appeared in 1923, it took the form of a light-duty truck chassis based on the new Superior series cars, on which buyers could mount a variety of bodies. Although the mechanical elements of the Superior Model B, as the truck chassis was termed, varied little from those of the 490, the wheelbase had grown slightly, to 103in, and the styling, with its taller hood, gave a more modern look. The one-ton Model T's replacement, called the Model D, was a heavy-duty model that also borrowed its engine and transmission from the Superior car. Two truck models seemed enough, and the three-quarter-ton Model G went the way of the dodo bird and other historical oddities—though the new one-ton Model D used its 120in wheelbase.

It's no coincidence that Chevrolet's early trucks closely resembled the manufacturer's cars. About the only difference between the sheet metal shared by Chevrolet's cars and trucks was that the cars had aluminum radiator shells, whereas the trucks used pressed steel shells.

For 1926 Chevrolet introduced its first pickup, created by placing a cargo box in the truck of either a roadster or a coupe. For several years Ford had been converting touring cars into pickups by eliminating the touring car's rear seat section and replacing it with a pickup box.

For 1928 Chevrolet unveiled its first sedan delivery, a model that would stay in production until 1960. This car-based commercial found buyers in a variety of delivery businesses such as cleaners,

Chevrolet used overhead valve engines from the get-go with the result that on a cubic inch basis, Chevrolet produced more horsepower than Ford. The famous "Stovebolt" six would be introduced in 1929, but in 1928, the model year of this truck, the engine was still a "four-banger."

Interiors on early trucks are simple in the extreme.

florists, and so forth. No complicated engineering was required to create this new model, since sedan deliveries were simply two-door sedans with metal panels in place of the rear windows, and a door at the rear. Deliveries came with only a single seat for the driver, but a second bucket-style seat could be installed for the occasional passenger. Collectors find sedan deliveries appealing at least partly because the cargo area affords ample space for folding chairs, a beverage cooler, and other comforts that make it enjoyable to spend a day or a weekend at a car show.

In 1930, Chevrolet for the first time offered a true roadster pickup. This was a specially designed pickup with an open cab in front and a full-sized pickup box—not a roadster with a box stuffed in the trunk, as the previous version had been. All sheet metal, except that for the rear of the

cab, came from the International AC series car line. In truck fashion, the radiator shell was steel painted black. Much is made over Henry Ford's supposed statement that buyers of his Model T could choose any color they wanted as long as it was black, but buyers of Chevrolet's early trucks fared no better. Until 1929 all Chevrolet truck models were also available only in black. For 1929 and 1930, Chevrolet painted its trucks Blue Bell Blue. But this single color scheme did not apply to the roadster pickup or the earlier roadsters and coupes with the box in the trunk, which were available in any of the car color options.

With the roadster pickup, Chevrolet nudged closer to offering a conventional pickup, which would finally appear in 1931. The timing of the pickup's arrival was neither late nor early. The cargo boxes on early pickups—namely, the Model T Chevrolet and the Model A Ford—were just too small for more than the smallest

amount of cargo. A contractor might give a foreman a pickup to drive to a work site, and the pickup might be loaded with a dozen or so shovels, but a much bigger cargo would be beyond the pickup's capacity. In this light it appears that Chevrolet had been right to sell its light trucks as a chassis on which a buyer could mount a utility body that best suited his or her needs. But as cars received larger, more powerful engines, and chassis length increased, a larger, more cargo-worthy pickup box could be accommodated. The result became the pickup we all love; a handy, carryall vehicle emerged that served farmers, owners of small businesses, and handymen (often as their only passenger-carrying vehicle)—and it would eventually become the hottest-selling model of American car makers.

While Chevrolet's light-duty trucks were gaining usable cargo capability, its heavier-duty models were making the transition to serious hauling. The move to a larger truck line came in 1928 with a new midyear model called the LP. The first half of that sales year, Chevrolet marketed its one-tons as the LO series, but really these trucks varied little from those in the LM line of 1927. The midyear LP brought a one-ton truck that was far more capable than any previously sold under the bow-tie logo. But for want of a stronger engine, the LP, with its four-wheel brakes and a four-speed transmission, could have been rated in the heavier-hauling one-and-a-half-ton class. In 1929 the new six-cylinder engine provided the needed power margin and Chevrolet upgraded its new LQ series trucks to a one-and-a-half-ton capacity. (Since one-and-a-half tons represents the dividing line between light- and heavy-duty, the LQ and its successors aren't discussed in detail in this book.)

GMCs

Today the GMC initials stand for General Motors Truck and Coach Division. Originally GMC meant simply General Motors Truck Company. Unlike Chevrolet, which originated as its own company, GMC resulted from a merger of two truck builders, Rapid and Reliance, which occurred when GM's wildly speculative creator William Crapo ("Billy") Durant added both companies to the GM fold. For a time GM continued to sell trucks under the Rapid and Reliance names, and these trucks used chain drive. In 1915 a new light-duty truck appeared under the GMC name. This truck, which used shaft instead of chain drive, became a popular platform on which buyers mounted a variety of bodies. With the United States' entry into World War I, the Army purchased 5,000 of these Model 15 GMCs, which saw duty as ambulances.

The Model 15's successor, the three-quarter-ton Model 16, entered production in 1920 and continued through 1926. As with the early Chevrolet trucks, buyers purchased the Model 16 as a bare cowl and chassis on which a body could be mounted to suit the buyer's needs. All Model 16s were powered by a 37-horsepower (hp) L-head four-cylinder engine and equipped with a three-speed transmission. No noteworthy changes occurred

The six-cylinder engine Chevrolet introduced in 1929 displaced 194ci and developed 50hp at 2600rpm. With upgrades, this engine remained in production until 1963.

Chevrolet's earliest pickups, first offered in 1926, were created by stuffing a box into the trunk of a coupe or roadster. In 1930, Chevrolet created its first true pickup by combining a roadster-style cab with a separate box. The result is one of the smartest-looking and rarest of all Chevrolet pickups. While other 1930 Chevrolet truck models were offered only in Blue Bell Blue, the roadster pickup could be ordered in any of the car color options. This example is owned by Dar Pace, Coral Gables, Florida.

The roadster pickup's passenger car influence can also be seen on the comfortable, attractive interior.

during this model's seven-year production run.

For 1927 GMC stepped out of the light-duty truck market, but in 1928 it reentered the light-duty arena with its new T-11 series half-ton panel delivery, which had been marketed as a Pontiac the previous year. The only differences between the Pontiac delivery and its GMC namesake could be seen in a slightly modified radiator shield, GMC nameplates, and a fuel gauge in the instrument panel. The T-11 featured a 48hp L-head six, a three-speed transmission, and four-wheel mechanical brakes. Besides the delivery model, T-11s were also sold as stake and express trucks. During its five-year production run, from 1927 through 1932, the T-11 saw a number of changes. In 1929 a Pontiac six replaced the earlier GMC engine. This six displaced 200.4 cubic inches (ci) and was coupled to a Hotchkiss drive, which replaced the former torque tube arrangement. For 1932 GM reverted to an engine of its own manufacture. This new engine displaced 221.4ci.

Although production of early GMC light trucks, particularly the T-11, was fairly strong for the period with 17,568 built, very few of these trucks exist today.

Chapter 2

Depression-Era Offerings, 1930-1938

Through the early thirties, Chevrolet kept its commercial line one year behind its car line in terms of styling. Accordingly, the 1931 AE series pickup utilized the fenders, radiator shell, and hood of the 1930 passenger car. Both closed-cab and roadster pickups were offered for 1931, and pickups of both styles were fitted with a steel box with wood flooring. This box would remain in production through 1934.

Light-duty trucks used the passenger car chassis, but the trucks did not have shock absorbers. Under the hood Chevrolet's famous overhead-valve six-cylinder engine now displaced 194ci, with the commercial version producing 50hp at 2600 revolutions per minute (rpm). The four-wheel mechanical brakes were cable actuated.

The 1932 Model BB pickup was distinguished most easily by the 5.25x18in

In the mid-thirties, specialty body builders were offering woodie station wagon bodies that could be mounted on a pickup chassis. While woodie wagons combined the cargo capacity of a truck with the enclosed passenger space of a roomy sedan, their wooden construction required lots of care. In 1935, Chevrolet introduced an all-metal Carryall Suburban that offered all the advantages of a woodie station wagon with none of the disadvantages. In the years that followed, International and Dodge both fielded similar vehicles, but only Chevrolet's Suburban remains in production today.

The bold art deco radiator ornament on Chevrolet's 1935 Carryall Suburban seems out of place on what is in effect a commercial vehicle.

drop-center wire wheels and 1931 passenger car sheet metal. Whereas early 1932 pickups mounted the gas tank under the front seat, later 1932s—those built after May—mounted the tank at the rear of the frame, as did the passenger car. On pickups and large trucks alike, the seat had a split-bottom cushion, which had been designed so that gas station attendants could remove the right-hand cushion to fill the tank while the driver remained seated in the vehicle. Chevrolet continued to build roadster pickups through 1932. After that all pickups were the closed-cab type. The deluxe panel delivery saw Chevrolet's first use of stainless beltline moldings—something that would become an industry standard—and also got the passenger car's chrome headlamps.

Chevrolet's light-duty trucks received a slightly stronger engine than the cars, at 53hp versus 50hp, owing to the use of a new Carter downdraft carburetor. The transmission now featured Synchro-Mesh and was identical to the passenger car's except that the freewheeling feature was not offered on trucks.

For 1933 Chevrolet's light-duty trucks received the 1932 passenger car frontal styling and carried over the cab and box. With the sheet metal from the passenger car front end, the trucks also received what the ads called stabilized unit mounting—which consisted of a rugged support brace that was bolted to the radiator shell

Chevrolet introduced its new truck models in mid-1936. Consequently, it is possible to see a 1936 Chevrolet truck that looks identical to a 1935, as well as those that are better recognized as 1936 models. Trucks with the 1935 styling are called First Series models, while those with the 1936 styling are called Second Series. The easiest way to recognize the restyled Second Series trucks is by the lower cab profile, hence the nickname "low-roof." Chevrolet was proud of its new truck cab, which featured a full cardboard roofliner that provided sound insulation and also improved the cab's appearance.

Chevrolet's most unusual early-thirties truck model was the canopy express. A 1934 example is pictured here. The canopy express was popular with fruit and vegetable peddlers in a day when it was possible to pull your truck up to the curb, roll up the canvas side curtains, and set up business. Ken New

and allowed the front fenders, radiator, and headlamp support bar to be bolted together as a unit for greater rigidity. Inside the cab, dash instrumentation consisted of three gauges rather than four, and metal trim panels covered the doors.

A very attractive feature of Chevrolet's 1932 passenger car had been the four chrome vent doors in the hood side panels. To cut costs, louvers replaced the vent doors on hood side panels used on trucks, though some deluxe sedan deliveries were fitted with painted hood doors. Under the hood the engine received a 4in stroke, bringing the displacement up to 206ci and producing 65hp at 3000rpm. For the first time, at extra cost, Chevrolet's half-ton trucks could be fitted with the four-speed transmission from the big truck.

During 1931 and 1932, Chevrolet painted its pickups and big trucks Blue Bell

Blue. This color was applied to the hood, cowl, doors, cab back panel, and box, with the radiator shell, body moldings, fenders, sheet metal, roof panel, sun visor, and wheels painted black. Nonstandard colors included yellow, orange, red, maroon, dark blue, apple green, gray-green, gray, tan, brown, and black.

For 1933 the standard paint color was Boatswain Blue, with the radiator now being painted the body color and the radiator, grille, and headlamps painted black. Deluxe pickup and panel models, which featured a chromed radiator shell, grille, lamps, double headlamp tie bar, and horn, sold for only $15 more than the standard models. Deluxe trucks also got shock absorbers.

1934-1935 Chevrolets

For 1934 Chevy completely restyled its light-truck line. Whereas the former pickup, panel, and canopy express carried the 1932 car line's boxy design, the new look featured rounded lines and a slightly canted windshield pillar. The result was a more modern-looking truck, in closer step with the competition—namely, Ford. The pickup cab roof now had a slightly arched

shape, and rounded corners softened the door window outlines. On the panel delivery and canopy express, the upswept curve that formed the windshield pillar flowed across and down the back of the body, where it ended with a slight outward rake. Apart from good looks, the biggest distinction of the new styling was that Chevy trucks now carried their own sheet metal. This was a historic first. From the beginning in 1918, truck bodies had been pressed from the same dies used to make passenger car parts. A radiator shell and grille appearing to be from the 1933 Chevy passenger car line preserved the new trucks' corporate identity, but as owners of 1934 and 1935 Chevy trucks have discovered, car and truck shells are not interchangeable.

Deluxe half-ton trucks featured a chrome grille and headlights, while these items were painted on standard models. All three light-truck models—pickup, panel, and canopy express—rolled on wire wheels, carried a side-mounted spare tire on the passenger's side, and were fitted with chrome hubcaps.

These DB series light-duty trucks used a longer, 112in wheelbase, and panel models gained additional load space by virtue of the engine being moved forward

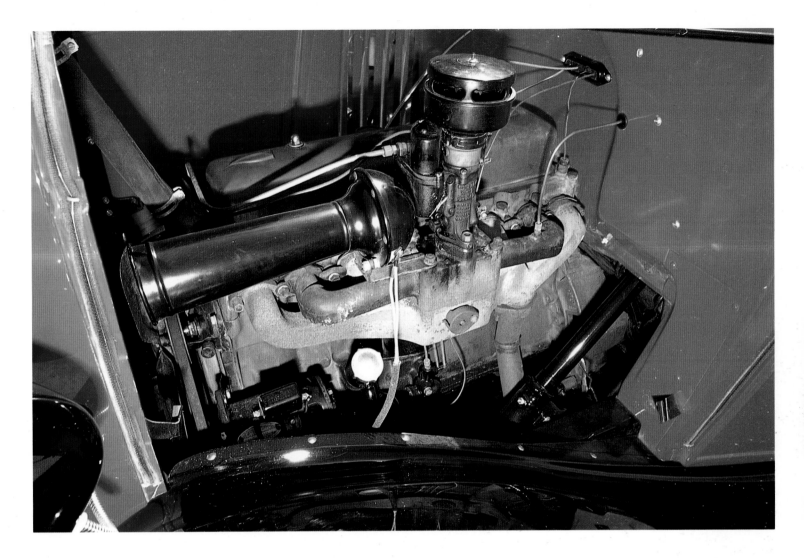

By 1935, the "Stovebolt" six had been enlarged to a displacement of 206.8ci.

on the frame. Options included front and rear bumpers, dual side-mounted spare tires, side-mounted tire covers, seat covers, and a heater. A canopy top could be ordered to cover the 72in long by 45in wide pickup box. All half-ton models were repeated in larger scale in the one-and-a-half-ton PA line.

Now called the EB series, all 1935 Chevy half-ton commercials continued to wear a grille-and-hood design similar to that of the 1933 passenger cars. The front bumper was now standard, though the rear bumper continued to be an extra cost option. Very few 1935 Chevy half-ton models are to be found today, since production of all body styles) totaled only 6,192.

The All-Purpose Carryall Suburban

The introduction of a new, unique body style—the Carryall Suburban—represented practically the only change to Chevrolet's light-truck line for 1935. The Carryall Suburban represented a significant breakthrough in automotive design. This was the first station wagon–type vehicle to be made all of metal. Essentially a panel truck with side and rear windows, the Carryall Suburban served many purposes, including: delivering goods to customers, carrying children to country day or private schools, transporting guests to resort hotels—to name a few. The Suburban differed from its closest counterpart, the woodie station wagon, in two significant ways. Its all-metal construction was much more durable than that of a wood-bodied car. And, since Chevrolet built the Carryall Suburban on a light-truck chassis, rather than a passenger car chassis, it had greater load capacity than most station wagons.

Although the Suburban's truck styling probably didn't appeal to everyone, what it lacked in grace it more than made up for in utility. With all seats in place, the Sub-

urban could transport eight adults in relative comfort. (The narrow middle seat had space for only two, leaving a walkway to the rear seat.) The middle and rear seats could be removed, and doing so exposed a 52in wide by 75in long load space. At the rear a station wagon-style tailgate and lift-up window gave easy access to the cargo area. When transporting a full load of passengers for short distances, such as when picking up travelers at a nearby train depot and delivering them to a resort hotel, baggage and trunks could be stacked on the rugged, chain-supported tailgate.

The Carryall Suburban's designers deserve a great deal of credit. Nearly sixty years later, this model is still in production, though today's Suburban can be equipped with a wide range of comfort options, such as front and rear air condi-

tioning, bucket seats, rear heaters, and
power windows, as well as many accessories, such as four-wheel drive, not even
thought of in 1935.

1936-1938 Chevrolets

Chevrolet waited until mid-1936 to
introduce its restyled truck line. A midyear
introduction would also occur in 1947,
1955, and 1988. In each instance, both
the older-style trucks (called First Series)
and restyled models (Second Series), were
built. This creates some confusion because
the owner of an early First Series truck is
likely to think it has been mislabeled and
actually is part of the previous year's production.

1936-1938 Chevy Light Trucks Firsts and Lasts

1936 Second Series
Final year with wood in the cab door
post, floorboards
Exposed front corners on the cab
Raised-diamond running boards
Last year with radiator cap coming out of
radiator shell
Headlights mounted on bars from fender
to radiator shell
Large, flat, screen-type grille
1937
Gas tank under seat; passenger's seat
must be removed to fill
Cab corners covered by front fenders
Headlights on grille shell
Same style grille as on 1937 car, but
truck grille larger, so car unit won't in-
terchange
1938
Last year of generator cutout
Relocated gas tank, with filler neck exit-
ing through rear cab corner on passenger's side
Heavier bumper with painted streak in
center

As would be expected, First Series
1936 Chevrolet trucks looked identical to
1935 models. The Second Series models
are immediately recognizable by a lower
roofline. Accordingly, First Series 1936
models are commonly referred to as high-
roof and the Second Series as low-roof.
Another major difference is the brake
mechanism. First Series 1936 Chevrolet
(and GMC) trucks continued to use cable-
activated mechanical brakes. Hydraulic
brakes first appeared with the Second Series. By the time Chevrolet adopted hydraulic brakes, the technology was well refined, so a hydraulic brake system from
this introductory year will perform to
modern standards if properly rebuilt and
maintained.

Light trucks in the thirties bore a
strong resemblance to the manufacturer's
car lines—even International, which didn't
build cars, gave its pickups automotive-in-
fluenced styling. As noted earlier, at
Chevrolet, trucks wore the car line's frontal
styling a year later. It follows, then, that
the new 1936 trucks carried the 1935
Master series passenger car grille. Lifting
the hood of either a First or a Second Series Chevy light truck exposed the familiar
valve-in-head six-cylinder engine, which in
these years was painted aluminum.

Unlike Chevrolet's practice in later
years, when it would build its pickups in
half-, three-quarter-, and one-ton sizes, for
1936 it produced only one pickup model,
rated at a half-ton cargo capacity. Chevrolet offering a single pickup model fit into
GM's corporate scheme, the aim of which
was to put buyers who needed a more
heavy-duty pickup in a GMC. The Chevy
pickup's 6-foot (ft) box with its wood-
planked floor carried a blank tailgate
stamping that gave no hint of the truck's
manufacturer. A chrome rear bumper,
which was different from the front
bumper, could be added at extra cost.

Chevrolet's other light-truck offerings
for 1936 included a half-ton panel delivery
and an open-sided panel offshoot called
the canopy express, as well as the Carryall
Suburban and two new car-based commercial models, a sedan delivery and a
coupe pickup. Based on a two-door sedan,
the sedan delivery filled the rear window
openings with metal panels and had a
door at the rear of the body to give easy
access to the cargo area. In front a single
bucket seat for the driver replaced the
sedan's full-width bench seat. Removal of
the rear deck lid and insertion of a stubby

pickup box into the trunk converted the
coupe pickup to a truck. Because the pickup box filled the space otherwise occupied
by the spare tire, all coupe pickups came
with a tire carrier in the right front fender.
The coupe pickup represented a Depres-
sion-era experiment in attracting buyers
by its multipurpose capability, but sales
never surpassed the marginal level. Low
production, plus water problems (rust,
corrosion, rot, etc.) that must have resulted from the absence of a trunk lid, make
the coupe pickup an extremely rare vehicle today.

Chevrolet's 1937 pickups, panels, and
Suburbans looked more up-to-date by
virtue of a grille that now matched the one
in the car line. Few would recognize this
change at first glance, but the 1937 pickup also carried a different box, now
stretched to a length of 77in, which would
be used until 1940. More radical styling
changes were seen on the panel truck,
which now had more rounded contours.
The Carryall Suburban and canopy express, which were offshoots of the panel
truck, also benefited from the more aerodynamic styling.

Perhaps the most significant change
to Chevy's 1937 cars and trucks occurred
under the hood. Over its thirty-four-year
life, the Chevy stovebolt six would under-
go two major redesigns. The first of these
occurred in 1937. Improvements included
raising the displacement from 208ci to
216.5ci, and increasing the number of
main bearings to four. The new block casting was 2in shorter, and the greater bearing surface plus shorter stroke increased
the engine's reliability—particularly since
Chevrolet continued to use a low-pressure
oiling system and poured Babbitt bearings.

Coast-to-coast economy and performance testing of a one-and-a-half-ton
truck generated excellent publicity for
Chevrolet in 1936. The truck even climbed
up Pikes Peak while carrying a five-ton
load. The company decided to attempt to
generate additional positive publicity with
more public testing in 1937.

Billed as the Second Annual Safe Driving Test, the 10,244-mile trip again
demonstrated the economy and dependability of Chevrolet trucks. American Automobile Association (AAA) officials selected
the new 1937 half-ton pickup for the test,
at Chevrolet's Flint, Michigan, assembly
plant. The truck was then loaded with a
1,000-pound (lb) weight, which included

a large placard showing the outline of the continental United States, wording that explained the AAA sanction, and an enlarged display of the familiar Chevrolet bow-tie emblem. As with the 1936 test, the route included a climb of Pikes Peak. Whereas the previous year's run had been more or less straight-line, West Coast to East Coast, the 1937 journey began in Detroit and circled the nation, with the truck arriving back in Detroit in an elapsed time of 328 hours and 31 minutes. Dividing the time into the distance gave an average speed of 31.18 miles per hour (mph).

Because of the time of year and the north-south, west-east route, the truck went through all weather conditions, from winter storms to tropical heat. Gasoline expenses for the more-than 10,000 miles of driving totaled $101, or less than a penny a mile. A total of 7.5 quarts of oil were consumed, and a 73-cent repair was made along the route. Oil was first added in San Francisco, 3,850 miles into the trip. No oil changes were made, but fresh oil was added as needed. At a time when other trucks—notably, those from Dodge and International—were better known for dependability, Chevy's much-publicized round-the-nation test of its half-ton pickup helped demonstrate the economy and reliability of its redesigned six-cylinder engine and the durability of its light-duty trucks.

As usually occurs at the end of a styling run, only minimal changes were made to Chevrolet's 1938 models. Most noticeable were a redesign of the grille, which again matched the one in the car line, with its horizontal, wraparound bars, and the installation of different hood side panels now containing three horizontal louvers. Sales literature for 1938 hyphenated the vehicle's name as Carryall Suburban, emphasizing, perhaps, this model's unmatched versatility.

GMCs

The T-11 model continued through 1932. GMC did not build a light-duty model for 1933 and 1934. For 1935 a light-truck line returned in two models: a three-quarter-ton pickup and a three-quarter-ton panel. Designated T-16Ls, these trucks used a 213ci L-head six-cylinder engine and had the same body styling as those from Chevrolet, with a different, distinctively GMC, grille and hood.

From 1935 on, GMC light trucks shared cab stampings with Chevrolet models, and the GM truck line also received the low roofline in mid-1936. Equally significant, a half-ton pickup model carrying the GMC label appeared for the first time. Identified as the T-14, it had a bed 1ft longer than Chevrolet's—7ft compared with 6ft—and mounted the spare tire in the left fender, as opposed to the right fender, which was the practice at Chevrolet. For 1936, 1937, and 1938, GMC light trucks were powered by a flathead six-cylinder engine built by Oldsmobile Division for its car line. Wheels on the light trucks also came from Oldsmobile.

GMC trucks came down their own assembly lines, and though their cabs will interchange with those from Chevrolet, GMC bodies were built by Yellow Coach—the truck division's body maker—and carried a metal plate so attesting.

GMC owners are known to boast that their trucks are meant to work harder than a Chevrolet. In 1936 this claim had some substance in fact, as the L-head six-cylinder Oldsmobile engine displaced 230ci, compared with 206 for the Chevrolet. The 7ft box, on half-ton models, gave the GMC slightly more cargo area, and its frame modulus was of somewhat thicker steel than that of a Chevrolet. Mainly, however, GMC's claim that it built heavier-duty trucks rested with its three-quarter- and one-ton models—load-rating versions that Chevrolet did not build in 1936.

Styling changes to GMC light trucks paralleled those on Chevrolet models except that the GMC grille had horizontal bars with a center "waterfall." Wide bars divided the grille's horizontal portion into three sections. These bars were painted a color that contrasted—dark or light—with that of the body, and the top bar joined the hood and cab reveals for a highly visible color pattern. Besides its half-ton pickup, panel, and Carryall Suburban, GMC also offered light trucks in three-quarter- and one-ton ratings. All used the L-head–design 230ci Oldsmobile engine.

Even fewer changes distinguished the 1938 models—the most noticeable being the absence of hood louvers and the addition of brightwork to the grille. The major change was under the hood, where a flathead six-cylinder engine from Pontiac replaced the Oldsmobile engine. The Pontiac six can be identified by the Indian-head crest on the left side of the block.

For 1939, Chevrolet trucks got a completely new cab that would be used with minor modification through 1947. Probably this cab's most noticeable feature was the split-V windshield, which could be cranked open for ventilation. Although Chevrolet's 1939 and 1940 light-truck models may at first glance appear to be identical, a couple of telltale differences are easily recognizable: the 1940 models had a wider band across the top of the grille and featured sealed-beam headlights. The 1940 model shown here, which is owned by Larry Hurst, illustrates both of these features.

Chapter 3

Pre-World War II Models, 1939-1940

Through the twenties and into the thirties, Chevrolet trucks carried the same styling features as Chevrolet cars—though truck styling was usually a year late. Economics aside, manufacturers have several reasons for not giving their trucks a carlike appearance. First, trucks are built to work, and handsome as it may be, car styling doesn't suggest a working vehicle. Second, cars are often fitted with delicate, expensive-to-replace frills and doodads that are a nuisance on a truck. Third, when a manufacturer builds both light-duty and medium- or heavy-duty trucks, they should ensure some styling continuity among the truck lines.

In the mid-thirties Chevrolet began to put emphasis on its medium-duty truck line, and doing so drew the light trucks away from the cars and closer to the big-truck camp. The first step in a separate truck identity came in 1936 when Chevy's car styling adopted a V'd windshield. Trucks kept the simpler flat windshield through 1938. Although Chevy's light- and medium-duty trucks both got a V'd windshield in 1939, the new truck styling kept well clear of imitating car styling. The updated trucks' most prominent feature, a tall "rib cage" grille composed of seventeen chrome bars that curved back toward the sides of the hood, presented a look of power and ruggedness—exactly the impression a truck should make.

The sharply V'd hood carried over from 1938 except that in 1939 the hood sides contained a single horizontal louver instead of three. To help carry off the bolder, more rugged look, the front and rear fenders arched 1in higher and the running boards stretched longer and wider. These changes blended with a roomier cab, which Chevy trucks would use with no noticeable external changes through 1947. To tie the new truck's frontal appearance together, a single belt molding ran from the topmost radiator bar along the sides of the hood, across the doors, and around the back of the cab.

Although Chevrolet dealers could brag to buyers that the trucks were "all-new," that wasn't exactly the case. Carry-over items included bumpers and hubcaps also found on Chevy's 1939 passenger cars, the same box as in previous years, and the 1937-38 dash with its three round gauges. Lifting the hood revealed the familiar 216ci stovebolt overhead-valve six. Although the Depression's gloom was passing, many buyers still sought to stretch a dollar as far as possible. To accommodate those who made thrift a top priority, Chevrolet offered an Economy engine, which looked identical to the regular 216ci truck engine but used different metering rods and jets in the carburetor, plus a throttle stop, which prevented full acceleration, thereby slightly increasing fuel mileage. Salespeople were warned not to

sell this engine in trucks that would be operated with overloads or in mountainous country or at high altitudes. Further, they were told to caution customers that performance would be curtailed. About the only benefit of the Economy engine was that it could be converted to a regular truck engine at small cost.

Options were few. Probably the most unusual was a canopy top that covered a set of steel stakes that fitted into the pickup box stake pockets. The canopy setup included weatherproof side and rear curtains. With this accessory a pickup could be used as a canopy delivery—a style of truck that was especially popular in those days among fruit and vegetable peddlers, who could pull the truck over to the side of the road, roll up the curtains, and be ready to do business. Why Chevrolet decided to offer this accessory—which put its pickup in competition with the canopy express model it built specifically for this kind of work—is anybody's guess. At any rate, the following year the pickup canopy set-up was dropped from the option list.

The new styling proved popular, permitting Chevrolet sales to edge ahead of Ford by a slim margin of only 4,137 units. This moved Chevrolet into a leadership position the company would hold onto for the next thirty years. Also during the 1939 model year, Chevrolet built its 2 millionth truck.

CHEVROLET PICKUP BODY FEATURES

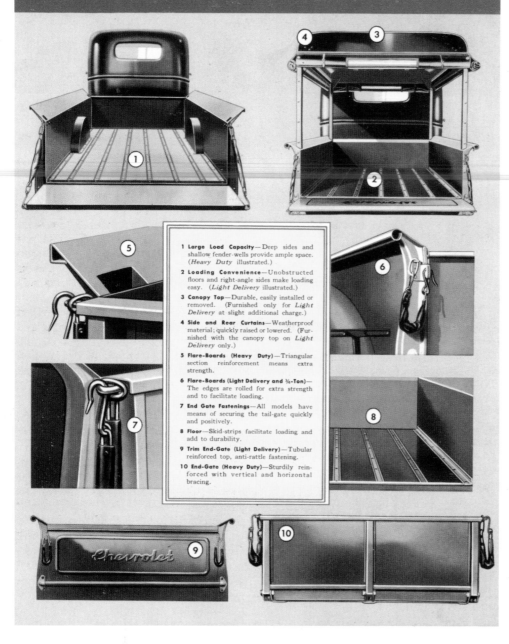

1 **Large Load Capacity**—Deep sides and shallow fender-wells provide ample space. (*Heavy Duty* illustrated.)

2 **Loading Convenience**—Unobstructed floors and right-angle sides make loading easy. (*Light Delivery* illustrated.)

3 **Canopy Top**—Durable, easily installed or removed. (Furnished only for *Light Delivery* at slight additional charge.)

4 **Side and Rear Curtains**—Weatherproof material; quickly raised or lowered. (Furnished with the canopy top on *Light Delivery* only.)

5 **Flare-Boards (Heavy Duty)**—Triangular section reinforcement means extra strength.

6 **Flare-Boards (Light Delivery and ¾-Ton)**—The edges are rolled for extra strength and to facilitate loading.

7 **End Gate Fastenings**—All models have means of securing the tail-gate quickly and positively.

8 **Floor**—Skid-strips facilitate loading and add to durability.

9 **Trim End-Gate (Light Delivery)**—Tubular reinforced top, anti-rattle fastening.

10 **End-Gate (Heavy Duty)**—Sturdily reinforced with vertical and horizontal bracing.

Chevrolet used two different boxes on its 1939 and 1940 models. The 1939 box was a carryover from previous years, whereas the 1940 box measured 3in wider and 1in longer, requiring all-new stampings. The canopy top, shown in this sales brochure, was a very rare and unusual accessory.

Although Chevrolet's 1939 and 1940 trucks were stamped from virtually the same mold, two changes made spotting a 1940 model fairly easy. At first you have to look close, but after identifying a few 1940 Chevy trucks this way, the thicker band at the top of the grille carrying the Chevrolet nameplate will be a sure giveaway. The other difference was sealed-beam headlights, which became an industry lighting standard in 1940. Since sealed-beams eliminated the parking light bulb in the headlight pod, the parking lights were placed in streamlined housings and mounted on the top of the front fenders. Parking lights on trucks were the same as those used on Chevy passenger cars for 1940.

Inside the cab Chevrolet's 1940 trucks had a different instrument panel with the gauges clustered around a semicircular speedometer. Like the parking lights, the new instrument panel was borrowed from the car line. Another change: a lock was now positioned on the dash directly above the glovebox. A ribbed stainless steel strip ran lengthwise below the instrument cluster and glovebox. This simple yet functional dashboard layout would remain unchanged until the introduction of the Advance Design series in mid-1947. Other than cardboard kick panels and headliner, all interior surfaces were steel, painted in a serviceable Thunder Gray enamel. For 1940 the steering wheel color was changed from black to Goodwood Beige.

For 1940 the half-ton pickup box grew 3in in width and 1in in length, giving an additional 2 cubic feet (cu-ft) in load capacity. By increasing the diameter of the rolled section of the flare boards from 1 1/4in to 1 1/2in and stamping the stake pockets from heavier-gauge steel, Chevrolet made the pickup box better able to stand up under rough use. The wider box meant new rear fender stampings, so while the front fenders will interchange between 1939 and 1940 trucks, the rears won't. Engineering refinements included a higher-output generator, required by the sealed-beam headlights, and a larger-capacity battery.

Chevrolet enjoyed another banner sales year in 1940, with truck production reaching 194,038 units, a 14.5 percent gain over 1939 figures and a whopping 19.5 percent edge on Ford's total.

Chevrolet Panel Delivery, Suburban, and Canopy Express

In an era attuned to personalized service, panel delivery trucks served a wide range of buyers, including plumbers and electricians, and stores of nearly all types. Since cargo hauled in panel trucks ranged from light to fairly heavy, Chevrolet offered this model in half-ton, three-quarter-ton, and one-ton ratings. For loading ease, panel delivery trucks were equipped with wide-opening rear doors. The driver sat in a bucket-style seat, with the space normally occupied by a passenger reserved for extra cargo.

Chevrolet's Carryall Suburban remained a unique offering. Although designed for hauling passengers, Suburbans could easily be converted for cargo by removing the rear seats, which were held in place by quick-release hold-downs. For passenger comfort in warm weather, the rear side-window glass could be lowered, and buyers could choose either panel-type rear doors or a tailgate–lift gate arrangement.

The canopy express also shared the same body as the panel and Suburban, with openings cut in the side panels. Flare boards with rolled edges stiffened the lower panel openings. This model functioned basically as a covered pickup truck, so a tailgate was used at its rear opening. At extra cost, buyers could option wire screening for the side openings. Trucks with wire screening were used by dog pounds and other businesses or agencies where operators wanted to keep live cargo from escaping or wanted to prevent passersby from helping themselves to items stored inside the truck. As standard equipment, all canopy express trucks came with roll-down side curtains of oiled duck to protect the load from the weather.

Car-Based Chevrolet Light Commercials

The coupe pickup, which first appeared in 1936, lasted until 1942. Today it's hard to imagine any practical use for such a vehicle with its pint-sized pickup box stuffed into what otherwise would have been the car's trunk. Probably the coupe pickup's best feature was that it came with a trunk lid for converting the car back into what it was intended to be. Not too surprisingly only 1,264 coupe pickups found buyers in 1939, and in 1940 sales fell to just 538, making these

among the rarest of all Chevrolet light-duty truck models.

Like the coupe pickup, the sedan delivery rode on the Master 85 passenger car chassis. With styling identical to that of a two-door sedan, the sedan delivery proved to be a popular seller among those wanting an easy-riding, economical, and speedy delivery truck. Production for 1939 rose 41 percent, to 8,090 units.

New among Chevrolet's commercial car offerings for 1939 was a wood-bodied station wagon. Woodie wagon bodies were available in either the Master 85 series or the Master DeLuxe with its Knee Action front suspension, which provided a comfortable ride. Although woodie station wagons are highly sought after today, they were built as utilitarian people haulers; at the time, a station wagon was, by definition, built of wood. The four-door bodies were made of ash framing with natural birch plywood paneling. A brown artificial leather material covered the top. In the truck's standard form, side curtains enclosed the opening above the wooden tailgate—with an upper lift gate available at extra cost. The station wagon proved to be nearly as big a sales flop as the coupe pickup, with production for 1939 totaling only 430 Master 85s and just 989 Master DeLuxe versions. In 1940, when the station wagon appeared in the top-of-the-line Special DeLuxe series, genuine leather seats became an extra cost option.

GMCs

Kissin' cousins, that's how close GMC and Chevy trucks had become by 1939. It was still easy to recognize a GMC, and owing to the stronger engine in GM's "up-

scale" truck line, GMC still could claim to be the premium brand. Visibly, the GMC's distinctive features included much thicker grille bars and General Motors Truck nameplates on the hood sides. The GMC script could also be found on the speedometer and the tailgate.

Beginning in 1939, GMC light-duty trucks used an overhead valve six-cylinder engine of 228ci displacement, which bested Chevrolet's overhead valve six in both bore and stroke and had full-pressure oiling with insert bearings. Owing to the engine's full-pressure oiling, the oil gauge on a GMC read to 60lb, whereas the Chevrolet gauge pegged at 30lb. The two GM truck lines used different oil pressure gauges until the introduction of Chevrolet's insert bearing 235ci six in 1954. Since oil gauges from a GMC will fit in the Chevy dash, a GMC gauge makes a good swap for a Chevrolet pickup that has its "splash oiler" 216 replaced with a full-pressure 235 engine. The GMC 228 engine is longer than the Chevrolet 216, so the radiator mountings are farther forward on a GMC; likewise, the headlights are moved forward with the radiator core support. Wheelbase lengths and all other mechanical components are shared with Chevrolet.

Apart from the absence of car-based commercial models, GMC's light-duty–truck line-up closely paralleled its kissin' cousin's.

In 1940 improvements of the GMCs matched those at Chevrolet: sealed-beam headlights, a new instrument panel, and fender-mounted parking lights. Except for a larger-output generator, mechanicals remained the same as in 1939.

Chapter 4

Art Deco Series, 1941-1946

The period between 1939 and 1941 marked a watershed in light-truck styling. International Harvester Company led the way with its bold, art deco–styled D series trucks, which were introduced in 1937. (Art deco represents a school of industrial and architectural design marked by bold lines and a lavish use of chromium. The Empire State Building in New York City is a classic example of art deco architecture. The art deco influence can also be seen in the sleek chromium faces of marquees on older theaters and Wurlitzer juke boxes.) Styling studies for the D series trucks had placed the headlights in the fenders—at the time, most cars and all trucks still used separate headlights, so this would have been a real advance—but separate headlights prevailed in the production models. Chevrolet, Dodge, and Plymouth brought out their restyled truck models in 1939, and Ford handsomely redesigned its light

The smartly V'd, two-piece windshield introduced with Chevrolet's restyled 1939 truck line gave a dramatic upgrade in appearance. But in 1941 the same cab, combined with a flashy chrome-plated grille made up of bars arranged both vertically and horizontally, made for the most stunningly beautiful truck of the era—and one of the best examples of Art Deco styling to come out of the forties. Besides the flashy grille, other styling changes for 1941 included flat-topped front fenders and headlights now peering out of of streamlined housings set into the tops of the fenders.

Cranking open the windshield on a 1939-46 Chevy truck provided plenty of ventilation.

trucks to resemble the company's car line in 1940. Studebaker, International, and Chevrolet again updated their truck lines in 1941.

Actually, Chevy stylists didn't create an all-new truck for 1941, though if you park a 1940 and a 1941 model side by side, the contrast is quite striking. In fact, the "turret-top" cab carried over from 1939, and new pickups used the redesigned box of 1940. The instrumentation and the cab interior also continued

from 1940. The big difference was seen in the dramatic front end styling with its glittering art deco grille; flat-topped front fenders; a distinctly truck-type bumper—formerly, Chevrolet had used car bumpers on its light trucks; and streamlined headlight housings that were now set into the front fenders. The parking lights looked out from their own wind-stream housings, which now perched on top of the headlights.

The new look was as up-to-date as a double-breasted suit. Chevrolet stylists had tastefully captured the art deco motif in both the wide horizontal bars at the top of the grille that swept around toward the sides of the truck, and the vertical bars in the lower grille section that curved inward toward the top where they met the flowing fenderlines. The bold new styling broke Chevy trucks out of their conservative mold and increased sales appeal.

With war looming and America finally emerging from the stagnation of depression, 1941 proved a record-setting sales year. Buyers of Chevrolet trucks chose a sound product. They must have patted themselves on the back for the decision to purchase a new vehicle in this auspicious year, as a few months later, Chevrolet civilian truck production ceased, and no trucks of any make would appear in the showrooms for nearly four years.

Besides the outspoken styling, a number of more subtle changes distinguished

Along with pickups, in its three-quarter-ton line, Chevrolet also built stake body models. This 1941 stake body truck, owned by Irv Neubert, former secretary of the Light Commercial Vehicle Association, was originally used to haul tobacco.

Unquestionably the most prominent feature of Chevrolet's 1941 and 1945-47 pickup models was their showy chrome grille, which gave these trucks a trendy art deco styling look. Most of Chevrolet's short 1942 production run had black painted trim, hence the blackout model nickname for these rare and unusual trucks.

a 1941 Chevy light truck from its predecessors. The wheelbase grew 1 1/2in, from 113 1/2in to 115in, with the increase occurring between the cowl and the front of the dash. The seat now adjusted to four positions for greater driver comfort, and a more comfortable treadle-type accelerator replaced the former button type that the driver pressed with the ball of the foot. Cabs will interchange between Chevy's 1939, 1940, and 1941-46 trucks, but this will create problems in authenticity. Besides the change in the cowl dimensions, already mentioned, the passenger's door lock on 1939 and 1940 models was in the handle, whereas on the Art Deco series, the lock mounted in the door below the handle.

Several changes also occurred that would increase these trucks' reliability, including a switch to larger-diameter kingpins in the front axle. Performance improved with a horsepower hike from 78 to 90hp and a boost in maximum torque

output from 168 pounds-feet (lb-ft) to 174lb-ft. Chevrolet's stovebolt six-cylinder engine retained its low-pressure oiling system and Babbitt bearings—a lubrication-and-engine bearing system that was outdated even in 1941—but it's hard to fault these Chevy sixes for reliability, and mechanics have compared their simplicity to that of a Briggs and Stratton lawn mower engine.

The most significant mechanical upgrade was the adoption of GM's recirculating ball bearing steering mechanism. Formerly, Chevrolet had used the worm-and-sector type of steering mechanism that could be found in most non-GM cars and light trucks until recent years. Comparison tests showed that 1941 Chevy light trucks equipped with the recirculating ball steering required approximately half the steering wheel pull of the 1940 models.

The half-ton line-up included the same models as in previous years—a pickup, panel, Suburban, and canopy express—and the three-quarter-ton line added two new models, a panel delivery on a 134 1/2in wheelbase and a stake body truck, and discontinued the canopy express. Because pickups are the most plentiful, they're the models most likely to be collected and restored, but the panel trucks and Suburbans are also sought af-

ter. Canopy express trucks of this vintage are almost nonexistent.

1942 Chevrolets

The attack on Pearl Harbor and America's entry into World War II halted all civilian car and truck production early in 1942. Chevrolet shut down its civilian truck production lines on January 30. Since various strategic metals, including chromium, were immediately diverted to war use, all 1942 Chevrolet trucks, except cab-over-engines (COEs), came with painted trim. Today these wartime trucks are referred to as blackout models. The correct color scheme for these trucks is for the grille, bumpers, hubcaps, hood streaks, and headlight rings (the parts that hold the headlights in place) to be painted Turret Gray, and the headlight rims fender color. Owing to the short production year, 1942 trucks are very unusual. The blackout trucks look very plain beside a shiny 1941 model, but from a nineties perspective, the painted-over brightwork looks acceptable, and in fact quite modern. The other significant change for this year was the deletion of the one-ton line.

1944-1945 Chevrolets

Realizing that farmers and vital industries were facing a critical truck shortage, the War Production Board in mid-1944 allowed Chevrolet to begin building a limited number of trucks for civilian use. This production occurred at Chevrolet's Norwood, Ohio, assembly plant, where military 4x4s and civilian-style light- and heavy-duty trucks rolled down the same assembly lines. These wartime civilian trucks differed from 1942 models only to the extent that the half-tons were fitted with oversized 6.5x16in tires and four-speed transmissions.

Chevrolet resumed full-scale civilian truck production on August 20, 1945, just six days after the surrender of Japan. After nearly four years with no new cars or trucks in dealer showrooms, a ravenous appetite existed for new vehicles. To make the changeover from military to civilian production as brief as possible, Chevrolet workers at the St. Louis assembly plant, where the contract for military trucks ended on Friday, August 17, 1945, immediately disassembled and removed all military trucks that were still on the assembly line. On the following Monday, August 20, the first 1945 model civilian truck rolled off the same line. These first postwar trucks were identical copies of the 1942 models, including painted trim, but they did not have the four-speed transmission that had been installed on wartime civilian trucks.

1946-1947 Chevrolets

Despite a several-month strike by the United Automobile Workers (UAW), during the 1946 model year, Chevrolet posted a major milestone, building its 3 millionth truck. Largely as a result of synthetic rubber and other new technologies developed during the war, Chevy's 1946 trucks contained several improvements over their 1941-42 and 1944-45 predecessors. These included better windshield and glass sealing, longer-wearing vinyl resin seat coverings, the use of oil- and age-resisting synthetic rubber in the water pump seal, and redesigned transmission

bearings. Other changes included six-ply tires where four-ply had been used previously; additional fender reinforcing to prevent cracking; and stronger, more rigid rear bumper attaching bars. A little-known fact: genuine leather seat upholstery could be ordered on all 1946 Chevrolet trucks, 3100 to 4400 models, and had been available in 1941 and 1942 as well.

The Art Deco series remained in production until May 1947, when the completely restyled and redesigned Advance Design models appeared. From about May 1947 to July 1947, Chevrolet built both its 1941-47–style pickups and the new Advance Design pickups.

(Some collectors find Chevy's approach of introducing a new truck series midyear, while simultaneously phasing out the old truck line, to be confusing. Yet this pattern has occurred four times: in 1936, 1947, 1955, and 1988. In the most recent occurrence, Chevrolet continued its older styling on Blazers, Suburbans, and Crew Cab trucks for several years after restyling its pickups. The easiest way out of the confusion of midyear model changes is to realize that for each of these transition periods, the old-style trucks are referred to as First Series and the new style as Second Series.)

In 1940, Chevy trucks adopted the rectangular instrument cluster also used by Chevrolet's car line.

Accordingly, due to the brief simultaneous production of the two styles, a 1947 Art Deco–styled Chevy truck is a First Series model, and a 1947 Advance Design model is a Second Series.

The Chevrolet Panel and Suburban

Along with its popular pickups, Chevrolet built four models of panel trucks in the Art Deco styling series—though no panel models were built from the end of production in January 1942 until civilian

Next page
Less visible differences: a 1941 Chevrolet pickup is 1 1/2in longer than its 1939 and 1940 cousins (with the increase occurring in the cab); the seat now adjusts to four positions for greater driving comfort; and a treadle-type accelerator is used in place of the former button type. As the accompanying photos show, Chevrolet's 1941 pickup looks good from any angle. The paint on this example, and modern whitewall tires, are not authentic. This truck is owned by Bob Garver of DeLand, Florida.

From its panel truck body, Chevrolet created three variants: the panel truck, the Carryall Suburban, and a unique Canopy Express. Although never a large seller, the Canopy Express found buyers among fruit and vegetable peddlers and others who wanted the protection of a covered cargo space, plus open sides through which to display their wares. Canvas curtains, shown rolled up on this impeccably restored 1946 model, could be snapped in place to enclose the side openings when the vendor wanted to "close up shop." Walter Deck of Ridge Farm, Illinois, owns this vehicle.

There's nothing shy or retiring about the look of the front end of a 1941-46 Chevy truck.

production resumed in August 1945. The panel models included the light-duty half-ton on a 115in wheelbase, a medium-duty three-quarter-ton on a 125 1/4in chassis, a three-quarter-ton model on a 134 1/2in wheelbase, and a heavier-duty three-quarter-ton model fitted with dual rear wheels.

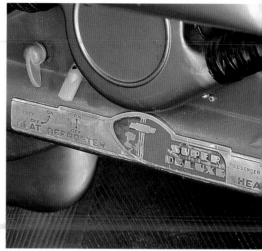

Since the forties were an era of functional transportation, accessories were limited to practical items. Collectors who want to dress up their trucks have to content themselves with adding items such as dual wipers, a passenger-side mirror, dual horns, or a heater like the one shown here.

These trucks featured all-metal welded construction with a tongue-and-groove wood floor.

A small difference distinguished prewar and postwar Chevrolet Suburbans. In 1941 the Suburban came only with the tailgate–lift gate. After the war the side-opening rear door combination returned. Suburbans were assigned different model numbers depending on whether they had rear doors or a tailgate.

The Appeal of the Art Deco Series

Although the Advance Design trucks of 1947-55 currently attract greater collector interest, Chevrolet's light trucks of the 1941-46 era are considerably rarer and also make desirable collector vehicles. The lavish chrome of the prewar and postwar models certainly sets these trucks apart, but their appeal also includes their mechanical simplicity and relative availability. Restorers will find that most hard-to-find parts are now available in reproduction form. Since this was an era of functional transportation, collectors who want to dress up their trucks will have to content themselves by adding dual wipers, a passenger's-side mirror, dual horns, or a heater—as only the most basic, practical accessories were offered.

Although the blackout trucks are less common, most collectors feel that the

Like the pickup, both the Canopy Express and panel truck had a wooden floor with skid strips for durability and easy loading and unloading of cargo.

chrome models have more charm. The extensive chrome speaks of an era marked by great events, of enormous heroism and sacrifice, outrageous cruelty, and courageous idealism.

1941-1946 GMCs

When Chevrolet restyled its light trucks in 1941, GMC followed suit, adopting the same body shell and a very similar grille. Besides the General Motors truck emblems on both sides of the hood, the easiest way to tell a GMC truck from its Chevrolet cousin is by looking at the grille. On a GMC the lower grille bars were horizontal, whereas they were lined up vertically on a Chevrolet. The other significant difference was GMC's use of its heavier-duty 238ci overhead valve six-cylinder engine.

Styling was evolving in the Chevrolet pickup interiors as shown by the dash of this 1946 Canopy Express. Note that the dash is rounded, not simply a flat-faced sheet, and it has metal trim and stripes running vertically in the center of the dash.

Chapter 5

Advance Design Series, 1947-1955

In the sixties, old-car collectors discovered the Model A Ford. Formerly, Model As had simply been ubiquitous; they could be found resting in junkyards, abandoned in fields and back yards, or working on farms in any number capacities, from home-built tractors to saw rigs, and some still served as transportation. Prices ranged from $50 to $150, depending on condition and the seller's hesitation. Model As were among the first special-interest cars to attract collector attention. As collector fever grew, Model A prices increased first tenfold, then a hundredfold. Soon the ranks of Model As formed rows at car shows, and even derelict skeletons vanished from the countryside. One wonders if today there aren't as many Model As in collectors' hands as Henry Ford built.

In 1947 GM unveiled its first completely restyled post-war model. Oddly, the vehicles selected to spearhead GM's leadership in the post-war era were trucks, not cars. Chevrolet built its highly successful Advance Design pickup series from midyear 1947 through midyear 1955. Although the basic styling remained the same, numerous changes occurred during this nine-year run that enable collectors of these trucks to quite easily identify an Advance Design truck as an early-, middle-, or late-in-the-series model. Although no identifying features distinguish the 1950 model, seen here, from a 1949, the absence of door vent windows (which appeared in 1952) place this truck in the early segment of the Advance Design series.

The dash on Chevrolet's Advance Design trucks is pleasingly laid out with both the instruments and the speedometer in round gauges directly in front of the driver.

If you've had your eyes open to the course of the old-car hobby, you may have noticed that collectors have discovered Chevrolet light-duty trucks of the late forties and early fifties with the same passion they lavished on the Model A Ford. Like the Model A, Chevy Advance Design series trucks have been ubiquitous. Most of us who are old enough to have liked Ike re-member the fleets of Chevy trucks that carried farm families to town, hauled building supplies, and worked in the background of every corner of our life. Although some are still serving, many are resting in scrap yards and other locations of abandonment. Today collectors are re-claiming these trucks so vigorously, from both active use and retirement, that you won't have to sleep like Rip Van Winkle before Chevy Advance Design trucks will have disappeared from the countryside as thoroughly as Model A Fords. Prices for re-storable examples are rapidly climbing in the $500 to $1,500 price range that is the customary selling figure of a dilapidated truck. Where in this range a particular example lies depends on whether the seller or the buyer blinks first—and restored examples are commanding upward of ten times those figures.

Responding to a growing collector interest, parts venders are duplicating sheet metal, trim, interior, and rubber items no longer available from the manufacturer, and the increasing popularity of these trucks at shows is igniting collector interest. The parallels are unmistakable: Chevy Advance Design trucks are the Model As of the nineties.

If you're not a truck fancier, you may have been wondering just which Chevy trucks belonged to the Advance Design series. Basically, these were Chevrolet's post–World War II models, built from mid-

An unusual and appealing model for collectors is the Carryall Suburban, which received a very rounded shape for the Advance Design series. Originally these trucks were purchased by schools and businesses that needed economical transport for up to nine passengers. The Suburban used a tailgate and lift gate combination at the rear and had sliding side windows.

Advance Design pickups were offered in two cab styles, identified as standard and deluxe. The standard cab had blind rear quarters, whereas the deluxe cab set attractive curved windows in the cab corners—giving it the nickname five-window cab. The deluxe cabs are especially sought-after by collectors, not only for their appealing looks, but also because they give nearly panoramic visibility.

1947 to mid-1955. Many old-car or -truck collectors don't realize that truck production resumed almost immediately after V-J Day in 1945, thereby gaining a several-month lead on car production, which did not resume for several months after the war's end. Trucks got a jump-start for two reasons. First, America's truck shortage had grown acute; they were needed and in demand. Second, trucks were already in production for military and limited civilian needs. The first trucks back in full-scale production were nearly identical to the prewar models, but in May of 1947, Chevrolet unveiled its all-new Advance Design truck series. Styling features of the new trucks, most notably the high-rounded nose and tall windshield, predated those of the corporation's restyled car lines by nearly two years. Although the new design reached more than skin deep—major changes were also made to the interior and chassis layout—the engine and the driveline received only minor upgrades.

Although strikingly different in appearance from its predecessors, the Advance Design series consisted of familiar models. Starting with the popular pickup, Chevrolet's light-duty line-up included a panel delivery; a produce peddler's open-

The pickup, Chevrolet's most popular light-truck model, found buyers in a variety of small businesses. These trucks have a reliability that is almost legendary and have become so popular with collectors that they are often called the Model As of the nineties.

sided version of the delivery, called the canopy express; a pickup minus its box, called the cab-chassis—this model was usually fitted for custom use, as in a wrecker, a firefighter, or a glass truck; the people-hauling Carryall Suburban; and a rare Cantrell-bodied woodie wagon. The heavy-duty Advance Design line-up featured dumps, stake beds, and semitractors, in both long-nosed and distinctive

and sought-after COE configurations. Most Chevy admirers are not aware that the light-duty Advance Design models can also, very rarely, be found fitted with very rugged and durable Napco Mountain Goat four-wheel-drive conversions, an option buyers could add by special order.

Even though the Advance Design series used the same body stampings all nine years, it is fairly easy to tell if an Advance

Chevrolet offered two cabs with its 1947-1955 Advance Design trucks. The standard cab, seen on this 1950 truck, lacked the rear corner windows found on deluxe models. Although a standard cab model, this truck is outfitted with several extra-cost accessories, including dual taillights (a single taillight on the left side was standard), whitewall tires, and fog lights. The rear bumper was a standard item on Advance Design Chevy pickups through 1950. This truck is owned by Ray Morrison of Apopka, Florida.

43

Design Chevy truck is from the beginning, middle, or end of the series. The 1947-49 models used screws to hold the headliner and door windlace in place; from 1949 on the windlace around the door was secured by a track. Probably the easiest way to spot early—1947-50—Advance Design models is by the absence of vent windows; trucks built in 1951 and later had vent windows in the doors. However, trying to date an Advance Design Chevy pickup or panel by this feature alone can be misleading, since the doors interchanged up and down the series and may have been replaced.

Middle-of-the-series models—1951-53—can be spotted by the absence of chrome trim, owing to the Korean War, and the substitution of push-button door handles in 1952 for the pull-style handles that were used through 1951. End-of-the-series models—1954 and the first half of 1955—can easily be spotted by a one-piece windshield and a wide, massive grille with center bars that vaguely resembled Chevrolet's bow-tie emblem. More precise identification can be made by the location of the gas filler pipe—on the right side of the box in 1947 and 1948, removed to the cab in 1949—and the design of the model nameplates. Also, if the truck is being assembled, dates stamped on the back of the heater and gauge clusters will pinpoint its age. The truck's production year can be found, too, stamped on the end of the pinion gear in the rear axle.

All Chevy Advance Design trucks could be special ordered with the panoramic-windowed deluxe cabs. The addition of rear quarter windows not only gave more visibility—by eliminating blind corners—but also made a truly handsome truck. Like today's pickups, Chevy's Advance Design series came in short and long wheelbases. All half-ton models used the short wheelbase and a 6 1/2-ft box, and

Suburban second seat passengers gained entry by folding forward the front passenger "jump" seat.

Dropping the tailgate and raising the rear window lift gate creates a huge opening for stashing cargo in the Carryall Suburban's load area. The tailgate can also be used to support oversized items extending beyond the end of the vehicle.

The Chevrolet Canopy Express

Although Advance Design series panel deliveries are fairly common, the canopy express variation of that body style is seldom seen. Designated Model 3107, the canopy express was based on the panel delivery body, though several changes differentiated the two models. First, and most visible, the canopy express had large, 62 11/16x26in openings cut into the rear quarters. These openings were covered by canvas curtains that could be rolled up when the operator wanted to display the cargo. Rather than using delivery-style rear doors, the express had a low tailgate and another canvas curtain to cover the rear opening. Inside, a bulkhead behind the driver's seat isolated the driver—and possibly the passenger if a companion seat was fitted—from the open rear cargo area.

Chromed front and rear bumpers were standard equipment, as was the toolbox located under the seat. Optional equipment included a governor, a chrome grille, a genuine leather seat covering, a right-hand mirror, dual taillights, heavy-duty nine-leaf rear springs, eight-ply tires, a four-speed transmission, and power takeoff.

the three-quarter-ton models had the longer wheelbase and a 7 1/2-ft box. Pickups were also available with a one-ton load rating, and these longer-wheelbase trucks were fitted with a box measuring 9ft.

Until 1954 Chevrolet's venerable 216ci stovebolt six-cylinder engine powered its light-duty trucks; in 1954 the larger and improved 235 six, which now featured insert bearings and full-pressure oiling, became standard. Since the 235 engine was an easy and common swap, it's almost unusual today to find a light-duty Advance Design truck with the original 216 engine. If you're wondering if your truck's engine is a 216 or a 235, an easy way to tell is to look at the pushrod cover on the side of the engine. The 216s—and 235s built for large trucks before 1950—had a pushrod cover that extended from the oil pan up to, and surrounding, the

spark plug holes. The newer-style 235s, built in 1950 and later, had a short pushrod cover that did not encircle the spark plugs, but stopped short of that area. Most likely, if a 235 has been installed in a pre-1954 Chevy pickup, it will be the newer, shortpushrod cover, type. You can also tell whether the engine is a 216, or a 235 from before 1950 by checking the engine casting numbers. All 216s from the 1941-53 period had casting number 3835849 on the block; all 235s from the 1941-49 period were marked with casting number 3693374.

Collector preferences among the Advance Design series are short-box pickups with the deluxe cab, chrome bumpers and grillework (where authentic), and accessories like a heater and a radio. Although pickup buyers were offered a limited choice of dress-up items, such period accessories as spotlights and sun visors were available, and these are also popular with collectors. The Napco 4x4 option, which was very rare on the Advance Design series, is also highly desirable. Chevrolet did not build its own 4x4 chassis until the mid-sixties. Instead, it listed the four-wheel-drive conversion engineered by Napco, a Minneapolis company, among the options. Either trucks ordered with the 4x4 conversion were shipped to Napco plants for installation of the front drive axle and transfer case, or these parts were shipped to dealers who did the swap in their shop. Napco Mountain Goat literature advertised the 4x4 conversion as so rugged that when the truck wore out, the front drive setup could be removed and installed on its replacement.

Collectors are turning to light trucks in part because of the popularity of trucks among new-car buyers. The reasonable price and availability of these memorable vehicles is also contributing to collector interest, but probably the biggest drawing card is how sharp these vintage trucks look as they're touring on the highway or displayed at shows. There's a timelessness in Chevy's Advance Design truck styling. With replacement parts readily available, light-truck collectors have had to contend with only one difficulty: finding a suitable alternative to the low rear-end gearing.

Trucks of the forties and early fifties were designed to haul cargo on a predominantly rural two-lane highway sys-

tem at speeds of 40-45mph. In today's driving conditions, cruising speeds of 40-45mph are hazardously slow, so higher-gearing solutions are popular. Apart from installing a modern driveline, the two avenues to higher gearing are to fit a higher-geared rear end or add an overdrive transmission. Since overdrive was not an option in the Advance Design series, this higher-gearing approach requires some engineering and driveline modification.

Unlike Model A Fords, for which collector value appears to have peaked, Chevy Advance Design trucks continue to rise in price. Show models are command-

---

Chevrolet Data Plate Numbers
by Rick Schissler

Since truck styling changed little from year to year, and license registrations don't always list the vehicle's correct year of manufacture—for example a truck built in October 1947 and sold in December of that year might be registered as a 1948—collectors often want to know if there is an accurate and precise way to determine not only the correct year of manufacture, but other information such as where the truck was built, the month of assembly, the original engine, and so forth. This information is found on the truck's data plate, which is located under the hood on the right-hand side of the cowl for 100 to 450 models, and below the instrument panel on all others. What follows are the keys to decoding the data plates for Chevy trucks from 1947 to 1954.

Suppose you own an Advance Design Chevy pickup with the serial number 5EPH2311 stamped on the data plate. The accompanying charts show that the first digit, 5, is a plant code standing for Oakland, California. The first pair of letters tells the year of manufacture, and the wheelbase and load rating. In the example the *E* indicates that the truck is a 1947 model and the *P* shows that it is a 116in-wheelbase half-ton. The third letter refers to the month of manufacture in alphabetical sequence—that is, January (*A*), February (*B*), March (*C*), and so forth. The *H* in the example serial number shows that the truck in question was built in August. Sometimes the month will be represented by numbers rather than a letter—08 for August, for example. The final four digits—2311 in this instance—refer to

the production sequence, which started with 0001 at each assembly plant.

The correct engine for this truck would be a 216ci six with an engine number between EP-1001 and EP-683120.

Chevrolet Truck Plant Codes, 1947-1954
1—Flint, Michigan
2—Tarrytown, New York
3—St. Louis, Missouri
4—Kansas City Missouri
5—Oakland, California
8—Atlanta, Georgia
9—Norwood, Ohio
14—Baltimore, Maryland
20—Los Angeles, California
21—Janesville, Wisconsin

Chevrolet Year and Series Identification, 1947-1955

Series	Wheelbase (in)	Vehicle Type
1947		
EP	116	1/2-ton truck
ER	125 1/4	3/4-ton truck
ES	137	1-ton truck
1948		
FP	116	1/2-ton truck
FR	125 1/4	3/4-ton truck
FT	125 1/4	3/4-ton forward control delivery
FS	137	1-ton truck
FU	137	1-ton forward control delivery
1949		
GP	116	1/2-ton truck
GR	125 1/4	3/4-ton truck
GT	125 1/4	3/4-ton forward control delivery
GS	137	1-ton truck
GU	137	1-ton forward control delivery
1950		
HP	116	1/2-ton truck
HR	125 1/4	3/4-ton truck
HT	125 1/4	3/4-ton forward control delivery
HS	137	1-ton truck
HU	137	1-ton forward control delivery
1951		
JP	116	1/2-ton truck
JR	125 1/4	3/4-ton truck
JT	125 1/4	3/4-ton forward control delivery
JS	137	1-ton truck
JU	137	1-ton forward control delivery
1952		
KP	116	1/2-ton truck
KR	125 1/4	3/4-ton truck
KT	125 1/4	3/4-ton forward control delivery
KS	137	1-ton truck
KU	137	1-ton forward control delivery
1953-1955 First Series		
H 3100	116	1/2-ton truck
J 3600	125 1/4	3/4-ton truck
K 3700	125 1/4	3/4-ton forward control delivery
L 3800	137	1-ton truck
M 3900	137	1-ton forward control delivery
1955 Second Series		
H 3100	116	1/2-ton truck
H 3124	114	Cameo Carrier 1/2-ton truck
M 3200	123 1/4	1/2-ton truck
F 3400	104	3/4-ton truck
G 3500	125	3/4-ton truck
J 3600	123 1/4	3/4-ton truck
K 3700	137	3/4-ton forward control delivery
L 3800	135	1-ton truck

ing in excess of $20,000 at auctions. Perhaps more significant to collectors, the $500-$1,500 entry prices mentioned earlier are rapidly vanishing. If you are looking for collector investment, this is the place to get in. Parts are readily available, and these popular collector trucks are supported by strong clubs. You'll find a late-forties, early-fifties Chevy truck to be a real enjoyable attention getter with comfortable cruising potential, and an easy platform for conversion to a modern drivetrain and amenities if you prefer a vehicle that looks old but drives new.

1948-1954 GMCs

GMC's first all-new post-World War II truck models reached dealer showrooms in the summer of 1947 as 1948 models. The FC series styling differed from that of Chevy's Advance Design trucks only in the

---

1947-1955 First Series Chevrolet and GMC Hood Emblems

For 1947 and 1948, the word Thriftmaster or Loadmaster appeared underneath the Chevrolet nameplate on the emblems attached to the sides of the hood. Thriftmaster applied to the light-duty trucks up to one-ton, and Loadmaster applied to the heavier-duty one-and-a-half-ton and larger trucks. The Thriftmaster and Loadmaster identification seemed too general, so starting in 1949, Chevrolet identified its trucks by a number scheme that related to load capacity. The hood side emblems were now changed to a number below the Chevrolet nameplate. The numbers identified the size and model truck as follows:

Series ID #	Size and Model
3100	Half-ton
3600	Three-quarter-ton
3800	One-ton
4100	One-and-a-half-ton short-wheelbase
4400	One-and-a-half-ton long-wheelbase
5100, 5400, or 5700	COE
6100	Two-ton short-wheelbase
6400	Two-ton–long-wheelbase
6700	School bus chassis

Owing to curtailments in the use of brightmetal trim, on 1951, 1952, and some of the early 1953 models, the hood side emblems had the Chevrolet name mounted on a bar, exactly as in 1949 and 1950, but without a number designation underneath. The 1953 and 1954 Chevy half-ton to two-ton models used a hood side emblem that consisted solely of the numbers to designate tonnage and wheelbase length. This emblem did not contain the Chevrolet name and was designed so that the numbers rose from a diecast base. Despite the use of the same hood emblem for these two years, it is easy to distinguish a 1953 Chevy from a 1954 by the grille design: 1953s still used horizontal bars, whereas 1954 trucks had the massive open grille with the single horizontal and vertical bars. The last Advance Design models built into mid-1955—known as the 1955 First Series—were identified by several changes including a completely redesigned hood side emblem. The new emblem consisted of a wing-shaped chromed diecast piece with the truck's series number in raised letters, inside an oval recess above the Chevrolet name, which was also created by raised lettering inside a recess.

As would be expected, GMC trucks used completely different hood emblems. For 1949, 1950, 1954, and early 1955, the hood side emblem on GMC trucks had the GMC initials above a diecast bar, and a separate three-digit series number below the nameplate. As with Chevrolet, the series numbers stood for load ratings.

GMC Series #	Load Rating
100	Half-ton short- and long-wheelbase
150	Three-quarter-ton
250	One-ton
280	One-and-a-quarter-ton
300	One-and-a-half-ton
350	Two-ton

The 280 one-and-a-quarter-ton model appeared last in 1953. Hood side emblems on 1947, 1948, 1951, 1952, and 1953 GMC trucks were not always accompanied by the series identification. Automatic transmissions also began to be installed in GMC trucks in 1953. If a 1953 or 1954 GMC was equipped with automatic, then the hood side emblems had the word Hydra-matic printed on the bar under the GMC letters. As can be seen, the hood side emblems are not a great help in identifying the year of a 1947 to 54 GMC truck. However, the features that set apart various years of Chevrolet trucks built within the Advance Design series—the appearance of vent windows starting in 1951, push-button door handles in 1952, and a one-piece windshield and more massive grille styling—also applied to GMCs.

distinctive rectangular-shaped grille and GMC nameplates. Light-duty trucks from GMC continued to use the Truck and Coach Division's 228ci overhead valve six and had a positive ground electrical system—Chevrolet used negative ground. In all other ways, these new FC series models were virtually identical to Chevrolet's Advance Design models. All sheet metal interchanged.

For 1950 the 228ci engine's horsepower output increased from 93 to 96hp, and in 1951 the engine was boosted to an even 100hp. A Dual-Range four-speed Hy-

dra-matic transmission became available in 1953 for all half-ton to one-ton GMC models. Other changes corresponded with those occurring at Chevrolet.

As on Chevrolets, the two most prominent features of 1954 GMC trucks were a more massive grille with side wings that enclosed the parking lights, and a one-piece windshield. In keeping with its up-scale image, GMC provided a chrome-plated grille and front bumper on deluxe trucks; standard models had painted trim. GMC's overhead valve six-cylinder engine now displaced 248.5ci and produced

The Korean War caused shortages of nickel that resulted in 1951- and 1952-vintage American cars and trucks having little or very poor quality chrome plating. The painted grille, hubcaps, and bumpers on this 1952 Suburban don't make it a plain-Jane standard model, but show it to have been built during the period when American car and truck makers were instructed to use as little brightwork on their vehicles as possible.

125hp. Unlike Chevrolet, GMC did not build a transition 1955 model; all 1955 GMCs had the new styling.

Chapter 6

Task Force Series, 1955-1959

The trucks Chevrolet introduced in mid-1955 made a radical departure from the Advance Design models that had been in production since 1947. As radical, in fact, as the change in the company's dramatic new car line, which went from stodgy, six-cylinder–powered predecessors to models with the peppy, optional V-8 engine.

Actually, in knowledgeable truck collector circles, when someone says, "I've got a 1955 Chevy pickup," there's immediate confusion because Chevrolet built two truck models in 1955: the older-style models called the First Series, and the new-style trucks called the Second Series. Here, we're talking about the Second Series, identified instantly by the rakish wraparound windshield, fenders integrated into the body styling, and "egg-crate" grille that always seems to look good on a Chevrolet and made a styling link with the new Chevrolet cars.

While everyone else still thought of pickups as a working man's truck, Chevrolet invented the "personal pickup" with its Cameo Carrier. Although the Cameo heralded many features not yet seen on pickups, such as the smooth-sided bed, in actuality, this model was little more than a cleverly disguised deluxe pickup that carried the same box as the 1954 Advance Design models. Fiberglass panels created the smooth-sided box illusion. Likewise, a fiberglass overlay and special latches made the tailgate look specially stamped for this model. This 1956 truck is owned by Bob and Linda Ogle of Champaign, Illinois.

Deluxe fulldisc hubcaps from Chevrolet passenger cars helped create the Cameo's "dream truck" image.

If ever a company had its "finest hour," for GM it came in the mid-fifties. It was during this period that Charles Wilson, a former GM president who had joined President Dwight Eisenhower's cabinet as secretary of defense, made his immortal statement. In response to reporters' questions as to whether his influence in defense spending would create a conflict of interest, Wilson flat-footedly said, "What's good for General Motors is good for the country." It was also in this period that the musical *Solid Gold Cadillac* presented the chairmanship of GM as the ultimate wish upon a star. Everything, it seemed, that GM did came out right. Certainly everything GM did in 1955 came out right.

At least one somewhat eccentric admirer of the Advance Design series trucks has deprecated Chevy's Second Series 1955 pickup as a "Cadillac in drag." Yet for the public, and most vintage-truck admirers today, Chevrolet's "new truck" look instantly made everything else with a pickup box look outdated. Some of GM's competitors, such as Studebaker and International, which had been style leaders in the past, never again came within sighting distance of Chevrolet after 1955.

Although many features of the Second Series 1955 Chevrolet trucks weren't new to the industry, they certainly appeared as a dramatic leap forward when combined with such radically progressive styling. For example, Studebaker had

Owing to the boxy shape of Chevy's 1955-59 Task Force series, the panel truck offered an extremely generous cargo capacity. For 1958 Chevrolet gave its truck line a mild facelift that is easily recognized by the quad headlights and parking lights incorporated into the vertical grille. Bryant Stewart owns this example. Courtesy Bryant Stewart

Here to stay!
Here to save!

with New Hustle!
New Muscle! New Style!

Stamina and stick-to-itiveness have long been a special stock in trade of Chevrolet trucks. And these broad-shouldered new Task-Force 58 models have even more of it! They'll keep on rolling a long

CHEVROLET

abandoned running boards on its pickups in 1949, concealing the step used to climb into the cab by placing it behind the door; Chevrolet did the same in 1955. (Ford and International pickups still had running boards until 1957.) Apart from styling, Chevrolet's biggest news for 1955 was its new V-8 engine. Since 1929 all Chevrolets had been powered by an overhead valve six. Although that six had been big news in 1929, reliability was its only claim to fame by the mid-fifties. Of course, there was certainly nothing new about using a V-8 engine in 1955: Studebaker had been offering a modern short-stroke overhead valve V-8 in its trucks, as had Ford. But besides being new to Chevrolet, the V-8 mouse motor—so-called because of its diminutive size—represented fresh engineering thinking in several respects.

Chevrolet's new V-8 followed a design pioneered by Cadillac in 1949 that significantly increased engine life and power potential by enlarging the cylinder bore (piston circumference) and shortening the stroke (piston travel) to the point where the bore diameter exceeded the stroke distance. Called oversquare, engines of this design minimize piston travel and thereby reduce internal wear while gaining a power advantage over older-style long-stroke —or undersquare—engines by their higher rpm. It's not just the short stroke that made the new Chevrolet V-8 engine more efficient. For the engine to reach higher rpm, fuel has to flow into the cylinders more efficiently and waste gases produced by the combustion process must be evacuated from the cylinders with equal speed. Cadillac achieved this improved "breathing" by placing the valves in the head, above the cylinders, rather than in the block beside the cylinders. But pushing the valves open from above the engine required an elaborate lever mechanism con-

Chevrolet promoted its trucks' assets as work trucks while continuing to develop their sharp styling.

A most unusual GM truck was the Suburban pickup, GMC's version of the pacesetting Cameo Carrier. Besides differences in the grille and nameplates, the GMC Suburban pickups also had the distinction of offering a Pontiac V-8 engine. This restored 1956 example is owned by Orville Abner, whose father bought it new in October 1955. Orville Abner

sisting of rocker arms, shafts to hold the arms, and pushrods to move the shafts. The breakthrough achieved by the Chevrolet engine's chief designer, Edward N. Cole, and his team came in the form of a drastically simplified valve mechanism that allowed the engine to breathe easier, consequently producing more power from a smaller package. Although critics scoffed at first at Cole's design, in time it would be copied by all American manufacturers.

Almost as significant as its development of the V-8 engine was Chevrolet's adoption, at long last in 1955, of open drive. Until 1954 both Chevrolet cars and Chevrolet light trucks had used an enclosed torque tube driveline. Although the torque tube design has the advantage of holding the differential—also called the third member—rigidly in place, it has the disadvantage of making clutch or transmission repair extremely difficult and prevents use of an extremely beneficial drive-

Engine compartments of trucks of the fifties are invitingly simple. Free of today's electronics and emissions-control spaghetti of wires and hoses, these vintage engines have everything in sight and are a delight to work on.

Color matching the interior to the truck's exterior paint scheme gives the Cameo an upscale look.

line mechanism called the overdrive transmission. Pioneered in the thirties by Chrysler and used widely by Studebaker, Ford, and Willys, overdrive offers the dual advantages of prolonging engine life and increasing fuel mileage. With the introduction in 1955 of open drive—which is also found on the First Series trucks—Chevrolet was finally able to offer overdrive as an option to its car and light-truck buyers. No longer did pickup owners have to trudge along at 45mph with the engine straining at peak rpm. Equipped with an easy-spin-

ning V-8 and overdrive, a Chevy pickup could now cruise effortlessly at 70mph.

As would be expected of an "all-new" truck, the cab interior featured a completely redesigned dash and instrument panel, new seat and door panel trim, and a large increase in glass area. The rather simple, though stylish dash featured an overhanging crown, which spanned the entire width of the cab and arched slightly to form a canopy over the instrument cluster. The upper portion of the dash panel was finished in a textured black paint to minimize light reflections, and the lower portion was color coordinated to the exterior. Instruments were located in a V-shaped cluster directly in front of the

steering wheel. The speedometer and odometer dominated the cluster, and the amp, oil, temperature, and fuel gauges (no idiot lights yet) lined up across the top portion of the V. If optioned, a radio would be positioned in the center of the dash, flanked by twin swing-out ashtrays—one for the driver, the other for passengers. A glovebox occupied the dash's right side.

The seat cushions and backrests were upholstered in an attractive plastic-rayon woven fabric. Foam rubber seat padding could be added as an option. The slick-surfaced seat covering made for easy entry and exit. Standard cab seat coverings had black as the dominant color, with beige trim. Cab doors used steel trim panels that simulated an upholstery lining by a raised embossment. On standard trucks the doors were painted beige for a neat and serviceable appearance. On deluxe cab trucks, the lower door area, below the removable upper panel, was painted body color. A small headliner cap of a black waffle pattern vinyl completed the interior trim.

Two-toned color schemes that had become so popular on cars were available for either standard cab or deluxe cab Chevy trucks. Standard cab trucks carried the contrasting color on the cab roof, whereas deluxe cab models applied the contrasting color to the window area. Bombay Ivory provided the contrasting color for two-toned paint schemes, in combination with any of the eleven exterior colors except Russet Brown, which used Sand Beige for contrast. Lavish use of brightmetal trim around the windshield and window openings, as well as a chrome-plated grille and front bumper, plus a full-width "wraparound" rear window set the deluxe cab trucks apart from the standard cab models.

With the introduction of the Second Series, two new models joined Chevrolet's pickup truck line-up. These were model

Next page
Although the dress-up trim that gave the Cameo a dream truck look appears borrowed from the Chevrolet's passenger cars, only the full-disc hubcaps are car items. The taillights resemble 1954 car-style taillights and a fancy rear bumper with a hinged center section that swings down to reveal the spare tire look like car items, but they're actually trim pieces designed specially for the Cameo. The example shown here is a 1956 model. Without question, Cameos are the all-time favorite Chevrolet pickup.

Unlike the nearly identical appearance of Chevrolet's 1955 and 1956 pickups, the 1957 models are easily recognized by a new trapezoid-shaped grille with a smaller trapezoid floating inside. Other changes included a flatter hood with twin "windsplit" bulges. Air conditioning was now available as a dealer-installed option. This 1957 3100 is owned by Bob and Debbie Higgins of Davie, Florida.

3124, a half-ton better known as the Cameo Carrier, and model 3204, also a half-ton but with the same wheelbase as the three-quarter-ton models and equipped with the three-quarter-ton pickup box. The long-box half-ton would become one of Chevrolet's most popular models and was intended for users who hauled light but bulky loads. Discontinued in the

new model series were the half-ton and one-ton canopy expresses. Chevrolet had been the last manufacturer to produce a canopy express, by at least seven years. Lack of demand finally did this model in.

1956-1957 Chevrolets

It takes a sharp eye to pick out the very minor changes that identify a 1956

Chevy truck. On 1956 models the side emblems were placed above the front fender crease and the spears on the front hood emblem were at the bottom.

For 1957 Chevrolet gave its Task Force truck line a front end styling update that consisted of a new trapezoid-shaped grille with a smaller trapezoid floating inside. Eight vertical bars—four at the top and four at the bottom—supported the smaller trapezoid. Other changes included a flatter hood with twin "windsplit" bulges, and reshaped fender spears with an oval-shaped relief containing the Chevrolet

The 1957 short wheelbase pickup shown in these photos is a deluxe model, recognized by the wide rear window and extensive use of brightmetal trim, not only on the grille and bumpers, but also outlining the windshield and used as a dividing line for the contrasting white color band on the rear door pillars and cab posts.

57

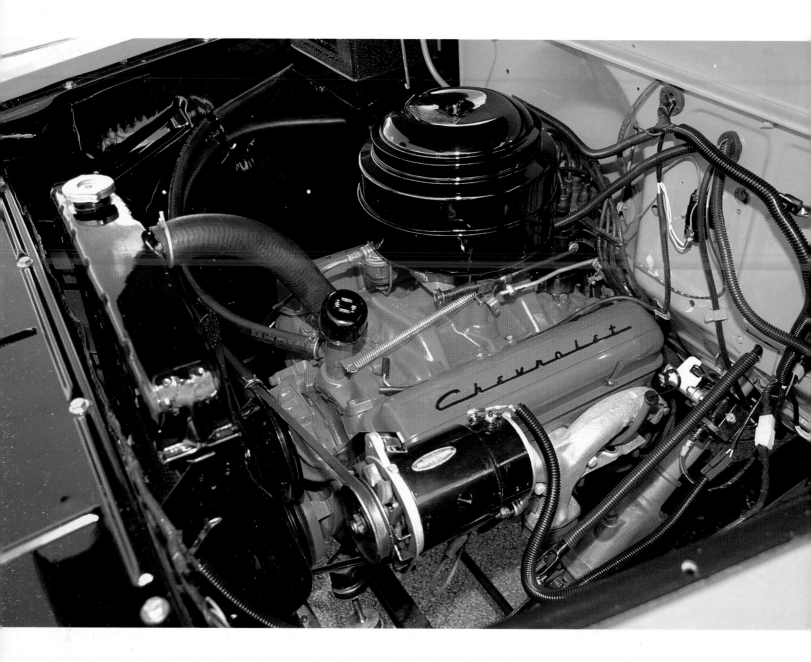

Chevrolet's small-block V-8, such as this one in a 1957 model, packed lots of power, enabling the rear end gearing to be lowered for higher cruising speed.

name and series number. The front hood medallion also increased in size. V-8–equipped models could be identified by a V-shaped emblem on the doors. Safety-type door latches became standard equipment, and air conditioning became available as a dealer-installed option.

1958-1959 Chevrolets

In 1958 the American automobile manufacturers discovered that four headlights would give greater highway illumi-nation than two. In keeping with its role as a styling and design leader, Chevrolet in-stalled quad headlights on its 1958 trucks. This necessitated redesigning the front fenders for a larger headlight opening. To keep the wide headlight pods from entire-ly dominating the look of the truck's front end, the grille was extended fully across the front of the truck and it carried rectan-gular parking lights, which were placed below the headlights. The Chevrolet name now appeared in the bottom grille bar. A new hood stamping with a deep, drop-center design and a slimmer, wider hood emblem completed the "new" look of the truck's front end. For 1958 only, lettering for the series name—Apache for the light-duty trucks—stood over the rear portion of the side trim spear, which also con-tained the Chevrolet name (in block letters on a black background) and the truck's se-ries numbers.

With sales of only 1,405, the Cameo Carrier bowed out early in this model year—to be replaced by the new Fleetside pickup, introduced in February 1958. The Fleetside was Chevrolet's first true slab-sided wide-box but did not represent an industry first, as Ford offered a wide-box pickup in 1957. Unlike the Cameo's box, the Fleetside box was made of metal and featured a tailgate nearly as wide as the box. To acquaint buyers with the Fleetside name, identifying nameplates appeared in the upper rear corner on both sides of the box.

A very minimal appearance change—namely, a larger and bolder front hood emblem—marked Chevrolet's 1959 truck models. Emphasis was instead placed on increased fuel economy in the light-duty series and an optional Positraction rear axle. Chevrolet's biggest, most significant truck "event" in 1959 came in the form of the El Camino, a high-styled personal pick-up based on the new car line. (El Caminos are covered in a separate chapter.)

The Cameo Carrier: Chevy's Glamour Pickup

By the mid-fifties GM dominated the automotive scene so thoroughly that the

Chevrolet phased out its Cameo pickup early in 1958 to make room for its successor, the all-metal Fleetside model. With sales of only 1,405, 1958 was the lowest production year for the desirable Cameo model. Dennis and LuAnn Justi of St. Petersburg, Florida, own this stunning '58 Cameo.

Cameos stored the spare tire in an enclosed carrier hidden behind the center section of the bumper. It's unfortunate that this tire carrier setup hasn't been adopted on modern trucks since it keeps the spare tire safely out of sight and protects the tire and wheel from dirt and road debris.

corporation's biggest concern was an antitrust suit that would split the divisions into separate companies. In this "golden age," it seemed that every engineering innovation, styling twist, and new model only served to boost GM's image as the strongest and boldest of the automotive giants. Chevy's glamorous Cameo pickup, built between 1955 and 1958, fit perfectly with this image and left no question in the light-truck buyer's mind as to who was the leader in pickup styling and design.

Despite the Cameo's "dream truck" appearance, it was designed for work—as the rubber floor mat indicates.

At first glance one might think the Cameo was a specially designed model, but in reality Chevrolet's stylists created it merely by heavily customizing a deluxe stepside pickup. The main customizing pieces consisted of full-length fiberglass fenders that gave the narrow bed a full-width look. Adding to the custom look were taillights that looked very similar to those used on 1954 Chevrolets but were actually unique to Cameo pickups, and full wheel covers from a Chevrolet car. A fancy rear bumper, also distinctively Cameo and totally unlike any other bumper ever used on any GM car or truck, completed the show-truck image. Constructed of seven pieces, the rear bumper's most unusual feature was a pull-down center section that hid a fiberglass spare tire carrier. Enclosed in its carrier, and hidden by the bumper, the spare tire was kept clean of road salt and dirt, and out of the sight of would-be thieves.

In keeping with the ornate use of chrome trim on late-fifties cars, Cameo pickups for 1957 and 1958 wore a wide chrome molding along the sides of the box, in addition to two vertical brightmetal moldings. Although it was unlikely that anyone would fail to recognize a Cameo as a Chevrolet, the designers still decided to attach a large bow-tie emblem to the fiberglass tailgate cover. The Cameo's unique model number, 3124, was incorporated into the front fender trim spears on 1957 models only.

The Cameo was unquestionably a pacesetter. With this exceedingly handsome truck, Chevrolet transformed the pickup from a beast of burden into a pleasure vehicle suited to occasional hauling. The Cameo's smooth box sides led to the wide-box Fleetside, and its numerous car styling features foreshadowed the El Camino. Today Cameo pickups are among the most sought-after collector trucks. If you're looking to buy one, make sure it is complete with all the Cameo goodies, since special Cameo trim and other features distinctive to this truck are becoming very hard to find.

The Chevrolet Panel and Suburban

Chevy's 1955-59 panel and Suburban models are gaining in popularity with collectors. These two versatile haulers shared the same body shell—the difference being the Suburban's side and rear windows, full headliner, and three rows of seats. Subur-

Chevrolet's V-design instrument cluster, introduced with the Second Series 1955 models, emphasized the availability of the new V-8 engine.

bans could be optioned with either panel-style swing-out rear doors or a traditional tailgate–lift gate. Inside, both the panel and the Suburban are extremely spacious, offering up to 225cu-ft of load space.

These practical vehicles are ideal for towing a show car or truck, hauling swap meet items, or performing almost any task you would ask of a light truck. Although Chevrolet designed the Suburban primarily as a people hauler (with all three seats installed there is room for eight adults), with the rear and middle seats removed, it offers nearly as much load space as the panel model. Of special appeal are the four-wheel-drive versions, available from Chevrolet beginning with the 1957 models. The higher road stance required for the four-wheel-drive transfer case gave these tall trucks an especially rugged look.

GMCs

Except for GMC's distinctive grille and front bumper with its two large cone-shaped projectiles, a V-8 engine from the Pontiac Division, and a distinctive instrument panel, GMC pickups and medium-

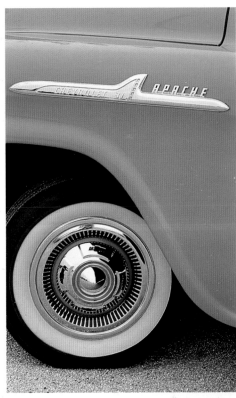

Up front, the 1958 Cameo was long on styling. In the back, it was ready for work. Ford, not Chevrolet, led the industry in offering the first metal-construction wide-box pickup with its 1957 models. Chevrolet waited until February 1958 to introduce its Fleetside wide-box pickup. The result was a handsome, well-integrated truck that captured the Cameo's charm and dream truck look, but was better suited to the rugged use of a work truck.

duty trucks for 1955 were little more than clones of Chevrolets. The grille, which was massive to the point of being ugly, bore some resemblance to the frontal piece used on 1954 and early-1955 GMCs—like Chevrolet, GMC also sold trucks representing both old and new styling in 1955. The similarity was particularly apparent in the way that the grille "wings" wrapped around the sides of the front fenders. The Pontiac V-8 displaced 287.2ci, compared with 265ci for the original Chevrolet small-block V-8. As had been the case on previous GMC models, the dash featured a full array of easy-to-read round instruments mounted in a chromed panel.

For 1957 the grille took on an even more cluttered look with a series of horizontal bars filling the center section. The new design no longer gave the impression that the front bumper was integrated into

Smooth styling touches were evident everywhere on trucks like this 1958 Cameo. The most recognizable differences between Chevrolet's 1957 and 1958 truck models are the new grille extending across the entire front of the truck and quad headlights. In the eyes of many collectors, no subsequent pickup has matched the charm of Chevy's Cameo.

the grille as had been the case in 1955 and 1956. On 1958 and 1959 GMC models, the grille reverted to a two-bar design, but the side wings no longer wrapped around the fenders and the bars were much less massive, giving these trucks a more handsome frontal appearance. The model designation now perched above the lower

bar. In 1958 GMC also offered a new wide pickup box identical to that of Chevy's Fleetside, though in the GMC line, this model was called, unimaginatively, the Wide-Side, and the old-style narrow box was the Fenderside. For 1959 all GMC models continued without change except that the two large bumper pods, which

had originated in 1955, gave way to a more conventional smooth-faced bumper. Most 1959 GMC models had painted grilles rather than chrome-plated ones.

1955-1958 GMC Suburbans

GMC's light-duty trucks for 1955 copied Chevrolet's model for model, including the Cameo, which GMC first called the Town and Country, then, for some unknown reason, renamed the Suburban. Confusion was sure to ensue between the fancy Suburban pickup with GMC markings and the Carryall Suburban with Chevrolet markings, but the name persisted through all four years of the upscale GMC Suburban pickup's production.

Although basically the same, these two pickup beauties differed in the same ways as any other GMC and Chevy pick-

Beginning in 1958, Chevrolet adopted a new classification system that put the light-duty models in the Apache series, the medium-duty trucks in the Viking series, and the heavy duty trucks in the Spartan series. The series name appeared above the front fender trim spear as seen on this 1958 Cameo pickup.

Unlike the Cameo, the Fleetside box featured metal construction and a tailgate nearly as wide as the box.

The cutout lines on the dash between the key switch and knobs reveal a king-sized ashtray.

Upscale accessories on this 1958 Apache Fleetside include a roof-mounted radio speaker.

up. Naturally, Suburban pickups carried the massive GMC grille—with enough gleaming chrome to blind drivers in the oncoming lane on a sunny day. As GMCs, Suburban pickups could be fitted with either the new Pontiac V-8 or the sturdy six. Other than these differences, the Suburban and the Cameo were carbon copies of each other, both carrying the same cab-wide fiberglass box, Chevrolet car-style taillights, spare tire hidden behind the bumper, panoramic windshield, and wraparound rear glass.

Napco: Chevrolet's Add-on Four-Wheel Drive

Most older-truck enthusiasts have heard of Ford 4x4 conversions made by the famed Marmon-Herrington Company of Indianapolis. Few truck enthusiasts, though, are aware that a Minneapolis company named Napco built four-wheel-drive conversions for Chevrolet and GMC light trucks, from the late forties into the

mid-sixties, when Chevrolet engineered its own four-wheel drive. When the buyer specified a Napco conversion for a new Chevy truck, installation was done either at Napco plants in Minneapolis or Detroit, or by a distributor, usually a Chevrolet dealer.

Napco literature used the name Mountain Goat to describe trucks equipped with its four-wheel-drive mechanism. The name was appropriate, as the all-wheel-drive conversion gave trucks so equipped nearly go-anywhere capability. Napco's sales literature also claimed its conversions to be the lowest-cost four-wheel drives on the market, and the easiest to drive. This may well have been true, given Chevrolet's cost economy and the engineering of the Napco steering mechanism. Other benefits of the Napco conversion included the availability of parts and service at over 7,000 Chevrolet dealers nationwide, and a 6,000-mile or 120-day warranty. The Napco four-wheel-drive mechanism was extremely rugged and re-

liable; some even claim it to be the best ever made.

Chevy light-truck collectors lucky enough to locate an operational Napco unit will find the conversion easy to make. The Napco 4x4 conversion consisted of a short drive shaft from the existing four-speed transmission to a two-speed transfer case, which splits power between the front and rear drive axles. The front drive axle is actually a Chevrolet rear axle modified with Bendix-Weiss constant-velocity joints to allow the wheels to turn for steering. A front drive shaft and a shortened rear drive shaft, plus a support bracket for the transfer case complete the package. No welding is required. Four bolt holes need to be drilled in the frame to attach the support brace for the transfer case. The Napco conversions can be fitted to panels and Carryall Suburbans as well as pickups, making these versatile vehicles even more useful. And beyond functionality, any 4x4-equipped Chevy or GMC truck is a great attention getter.

This gleaming black Apache Fleetside illustrates several 1958 styling features including the prominent hood and side fender emblems. The interior upholstery and the exhaust tips of this 1958 Apache are not stock. This truck is owned by Ralph Westcott of Largo, Florida, and since it has a V-8 engine, it uses key starting, not a toe starter button as would be found on a '58 truck with a six-cylinder engine.

Chapter 7

Aircraft-Inspired Models, 1960-1966

The wild, aircraft-inspired styling that swept across GM's car lines in 1959 appeared in the Chevy and GMC trucks of 1960. It doesn't take too much imagination to see the air intakes of a jet fighter in the "cat's-eye" pods boldly fronting the hood of a 1960 (and 1961) GM truck. Also like GM's cars, which now had a profile lower than that of all but a few European sports sedans, the new pickups had an overall height that had descended a full 7in Chevy designers applied a couple of familiar hot rodder tricks in lowering the 1960 trucks. First, they redesigned the frame around a drop-center cross-member, and then they chopped and flattened the cab roof. This lowered the new Chevy and GMC trucks in two measurements: overall, from the top of the cab to the pavement, and inside, from the top of the seat to the ground. Putting the seat closer to the ground helped reduce that awkward stretch required when climbing up into the cab, something that had been particularly irksome to women.

Just because the new trucks were lower didn't mean they were smaller. Despite

The lower, wider styling on Chevrolet's 1960-66 pickup has a crisp, modern look. Although trucks from this styling series used the same cab and pickup box, the earlier 1960-63 models featured the wrap-around windshield seen on this 1961 example. This 1961 Apache is owned by Paul Garlick of Lehigh Acres, Florida.

For 1961, the Chevrolet name appeared on a bar in the center of the grille.

the chopped roofline, headroom increased by 1 3/10in, and cab width and roominess expanded as well. The glass area increased, too, with the new pano-

ramic windshield boosting front and side visibility by 263 square inches (sq in) over that of the 1959 models.

GM didn't lower, lengthen, and widen its new trucks just for appearance. The greater length gave more cargo room in the box, and the expanded width meant not only more comfortable seating, but also a wider load capacity—on pickups fitted with the Fleetside box. Positioning the chassis closer to the ground and dropping the cab height also resulted in improved cornering and handling, especially when the the truck was driven unloaded. Thanks to a sharply indented waistline, GM's Fleetside pickups avoided the "appliance" look of Ford's 1957-60 Styleside light-duty trucks.

Although the styling changes gave the image of important advances, the really significant modifications caught most truck buyers by surprise. In 1960, six years ahead of Ford, Chevrolet introduced an independent front suspension (IFS) torsion bar front end. Actually, GM redesigned its light-truck suspension at both ends. Up front, A-arm independent suspension with rugged torsion bars, rather than coil springs as found on GM's automotive front suspensions, replaced the former beam axle. The new suspension also incorporated ball joints, which generate less friction, thereby reducing steering effort—a significant improvement at a time when power steering was not common on light

Model C1434 Fleetside Pickup

odel C3604 Stepside Pickup

Totally new for 1960...

Sparkling New Models — Pickups, Panels, Stakes, Suburban Carryalls and Chassis-Cabs — with revolutionary new ride, style and ruggedness!

In Chevy's big new light-duty lineup, covering the field from busy 6½-foot pickups through hard-working 12-foot stakes, you're sure to find the one best truck for your job! Pickups are offered in three sizes, with GVW's up to 7,800 lbs.; there are both sleek, high-capacity Fleetside models and

Of all of Chevy's light-duty models in the 1960-66 series, the Carryall Suburban wore the squared-off styling best. With the roof painted a contrasting color, as seen in this example, the Suburban actually looked like a pickup with a full cap over the box. This Suburban's only drawback was the absence of rear side doors. Owing to the low overall height, rear seat passengers had to bend nearly double as they crawled their way back to their seat.

Chevrolet's ad claims that its 1960 trucks were totally new were about 95 percent accurate. Virtually everything about these trucks, except the engines, transmissions, and rear axles, were, in fact, all-new designs. Not only did the new styling

carry the aircraft motif introduced in a striking way with GM's 1959 car lines, but of more significance, GM's trucks for the first time offered a carlike ride thanks to IFS.

trucks. At the rear Chevy's light trucks rode on coil springs. One drawback to leaf springs, particularly on a truck, is that dirt and rust collect between the spring leaves, causing the springs to bind and resulting in a harsh, noisy ride. Since coil springs have no metal-to-metal contact, there's no binding and the springs stay flexible throughout the truck's life.

Although the cab, Fleetside box, and chassis design were all new, engine and drivetrain selections remained unchanged from those in preceding years. And for good reason: Chevy's powertrain offerings were hard to beat. The standard 235ci Thriftmaster six represented a refined, pressure-lubricated version of the 216 six. Owners loved this engine for its simplicity—it was about as easy to work on as a Briggs and Stratton lawn mower engine—and its near indestructibility in hard service. A slightly detuned version of the 235 six, called the Thriftmaster Economy option, rated at 110hp, could be ordered on the C-10 series. The extra-cost 283ci Trademaster V-8 also qualified as a winner. Weighing less than the six, this high-

revving short-stroke V-8 combined virtually unmatched reliability with abundant performance. Transmission choices included the standard three-speed, optional heavy-duty three- and four-speed manual gearboxes, and a two-speed Powerglide automatic. With either the standard 3.9:1 rear axle ratio or the optional 3.38:1 ratio, these trucks cruised easily at highway speeds.

Chevrolet now offered its light-duty trucks in two trim packages: Deluxe (standard) and Custom. Externally, the Custom cab package was recognized by a chrome grille and hubcaps, plated vent pane and door glass frames, a bright windshield molding and upper rear quarter "scalp" molding, and a brightmetal beltline molding with the word Custom in black script. Inside, both cabs featured a silver-and-charcoal color scheme with body metal painted silver and a mixture of silver and charcoal coloring on the instrument panel and seat coverings. The Deluxe cab featured a single sunshade and vinyl upholstery. The Custom cab had a much dressier look with simulated trim on the door panels, a left-door armrest made up of a silver vinyl top and a black plastic base, cloth seats with charcoal vinyl fac-

Deluxe pickup models such as this 1960 model now offered two-toned paint schemes that applied contrasting colors to the lower body as well as the roof cap. The lower look of trucks in this styling series is more than illusion. Chevrolet's 1960 half-ton pickup measured a full 7in lower overall than the 1959 models.

ings and extra foam padding, chrome dash knobs, and a chromed Chevrolet nameplate on the dash. Buyers who ordered the Custom cab option also received a passenger's-side sunshade, a cigar lighter, and a left-side door lock.

Prominent styling features of the 1960-66 Chevy light trucks, besides the lowered profile, included the headlight location just above the bumper, and the parking lights set high into the hood—a reversal of the headlight and parking light positions on the 1958-59 models. As in 1958 and 1959, the Chevrolet name appeared in black letters stamped into the bottom grille bar. On the hood crest between the parking light pods, Chevrolet

placed an emblem indicating engine choice: trucks equipped with the sturdy six carried a bow-tie emblem painted red; on V-8–powered trucks, the bow tie sat in a widespread *V*.

Besides the C—for "conventional"—series light trucks, Chevrolet also built K series four-wheel-drive pickups and Carryall Suburbans in the half-ton and three-quarter-ton load ranges. Through 1966 Chevrolet's four-wheel-drive apparatus continued to be built by Napco, and these add-on four-wheel-drives had a distinctively high stance that resulted from a need to elevate the chassis in order for the front drive shaft to clear the transmission support member. Collectors who own a late-

Frugal truck buyers still preferred the familiar six-cylinder engine.

fifties or early-sixties Chevy four-wheel-drive will be interested to know that the model number, axle ratio, and production date are stamped on the drain boss on the left side of the transfer case.

1961 Chevrolets

The easiest way to spot a 1961 was by the styling changes in the grille and in the parking light pods. Now the Chevrolet nameplate could be found in the center of the grille, where it replaced the former vertical bars, and "wings" instead of air slots

69

flanked the parking lights. For 1961 truck hubcaps had a flat center section stamped with the bow-tie emblem; the 1960 models had cone-shaped hubcaps. Engine and driveline specifications stayed the same, but Chevrolet discontinued the Thriftmaster Economy option.

1962 Chevrolets

Automotive styling in the sixties returned to more functional lines and less emphasis on glitz and glitter. To give its trucks a more straightforward look,

Durable yet attractive interiors appealed to buyers who thought of their truck as a "second car."

Chevrolet eliminated the cat's-eye pods in the front of the hood, replaced the former quad headlights with a pair of single lights, and set the parking lights in plain, rectangular housings. Simple as these changes were, they substantially altered the truck's appearance. The Chevrolet name returned to the bottom grille bar, and an uncluttered grid insert, consisting of two horizontal and two vertical slats, filled the grille opening.

1963 Chevrolets

The easiest way to differentiate Chevy's 1962 and 1963 light trucks is by the grille. For 1963 the headlights peered

The jet aircraft motif that clearly influenced the styling of Chevrolet's 1959 car line can also be seen in the "intake pods" formed around the parking lights set into the leading edge of the hood. (Nonstock items on this truck include the modern radial tires and the small "Overdrive" tailgate emblem.)

The traditional narrow stepside pickup box has remained popular with new truck buyers and collectors alike. Chevrolet used the same rear fenders from 1955 to 1966 and kept the same box into the eighties. The result is better parts availability that makes stepside pickups much easier to restore than wide-box Fleetside models. Fred Skaggs of Ft. Lauderdale, Florida, owns this 1963 C10.

out from round pods, as opposed to the larger oval headlight housings used in 1962, and the grille spanned the entire distance between the headlights. Other, less noticeable changes included the relocation of the series insignia from the upper cowl to the front quarter panel, plus a restyled front bumper.

The big news for 1963 came in the form of an all-new coil spring front suspension that replaced the expensive-to-build torsion bar setup. Although the torsion bar suspension had been used on all Chevrolet trucks—up through the heavy-duty 80 series—only the light-duty models benefited from the new coil spring layout;

the big trucks returned to a beam axle and leaf springs. Since the coil spring front suspension eliminated the need for a heavy cross-braced frame, Chevy's light trucks returned to a less expensive ladder frame chassis arrangement. The rear suspension was also redesigned, and it now incorporated two-stage rear coil springs consisting of tightly wound center coils designed to compress under a load and more loosely wrapped outer coils positioned to preserve spring flex.

Many Chevy truck buyers in 1963 must have experienced mild surprise when they opened the hood and found a new-design High Torque six replacing the familiar stovebolt engine. This new six featured a seven-main bearing crankshaft,

The 1963 pickup seen here represents the second stage of a subtle styling evolution that occurred during Chevrolet's 1960 to 66 model run. This was the last year for the wrap-around windshield that originated with the 1960 models, the second year of the revised hood that omitted the "jet intake" headlight pods of the 1960 to 61 models, and the first year of the full-width wire-mesh grills that would continue to be used through 1966.

As pickup sales increased, the interiors grew increasingly attractive with brighter colors and more intricately patterned vinyl seat coverings.

and it shared pistons, rods, crankshaft bearings, and the lightweight rocker arm design with Chevrolet's popular small-block V-8. The redesigned six is most easily spotted by its narrower rocker arm cover. Also, 1963 marked the year Chevrolet trucks adopted alternators in place of generators.

Chevrolet was now selling one truck for every six cars. By contrast, in 1918, the year Chevrolet introduced its truck line, the ratio was one truck to every 104 cars.

1964 Chevrolets

Replacing the wraparound windshield with a one-piece slanted windshield gave Chevrolet's trucks a substantially cleaner look for 1964. Other changes included a slightly reworked grille with smaller openings and square, rather than rounded, headlight pods. The Chevrolet name moved to the top grille bar, where it remained through the end of this styling series.

1965-1966 Chevrolets

It takes a trained eye to tell the 1964 and 1965 Chevy pickups apart. Practically the only observable difference was a redesigned emblem, now of vertical rather than horizontal shape, which sat higher on the cowl. Differences are equally hard to spot between Chevy's 1965 and 1966 light-truck models. For the final year of this series, the side emblem took a rectangular shape and was once again located on the front quarter panel. The real problem is to distinguish a 1964 from a 1966 Chevy truck, because both had the side emblems in the same location. You'll have to look carefully, but if you do, you'll see that the 1964 model designation is capped by a bow tie, whereas on the 1966, the bow-tie insignia is incorporated into the emblem.

Trucks in general passed a major milestone in 1965. For the first time in history, sales of all US makes of trucks rated at under 6000lb gross vehicle weight (GVW) surpassed a million units. In 1966 Chevy's light-truck production passed 600,000 units, and in the process, Chevrolet built its 10 millionth truck.

The Chevrolet Panel and Suburban

Both the Chevrolet panel and the Chevrolet Carryall Suburban closely resembled pickups fitted with a soon-to-become-popular box cap. A ridge across the roof, in line with the end of the front doors, helped emphasize this box cap illusion. When panel and Suburban models were two-toned, the front roof section, cab pillars, hood, and body midriff were painted ivory, and the aft roof section, side window pillars, area surrounding the rear window or windows, and the lower body were painted the specified body color.

1960-1961 GMCs

GMC joined Chevrolet with totally new truck styling for 1960, including torsion bar IFS and coil springs at the rear. Differences from previous years' models were seen in the distinctive grille treatment featuring one large horizontal bar with the GMC logo floating below and an all-new V-6 engine, a GMC exclusive—the 269.5ci in-line six powered only GMC's van and parcel delivery models. The engine produced 150hp at 3600rpm and 260lb-ft of torque from 304.7ci, and boasted the shortest stroke of any six-cylinder engine.

1962-1963 GMCs

GMC trucks received the same redesigned front end treatment as Chevrolets. Overall styling, mechanical specifications, and model line-ups continued to be the same as Chevrolet's, except that GMC did not market the Corvair-based commercial vehicles. For 1963 GMC dropped its inline six, which it replaced with two engines from Chevrolet: a 153ci overhead valve six, used in the smallest GMC delivery, and a 230ci overhead valve six, powering the larger vans.

At the factory, Chevrolet pickup flooring was given a dull black coating. It takes a lot of restraint for a restorer to paint his truck's new bedwood somber black instead of applying a glistening varnish.

Although in 1955 wraparound windshields were the biggest fad in automotive styling since tail fins, by the mid-sixties the visual distortions produced by the sharply angled windshield corners led to a return to more mildly curved windshield glass. Chevrolet made the switch from wraparound windshields on its pickups in 1964. Very few styling changes occurred from that point until the end of the styling series in 1966. However, sales continued to climb and in 1966 sales of Chevrolet pickups exceeded 600,000, a record. That put the total number of Chevrolet trucks sold over the 10 million mark.

Chevrolet identified trucks equipped with the Custom trim package by a brightmetal band attached to the rear cab pillar.

1964 GMCs

GMC abandoned the panoramic-type windshield for 1964. Also, the GMC line-up added two new models, the Handi-Van and the Handi-Bus, both borrowed from Chevrolet. Customer dissatisfaction with

By 1966 Chevrolet's small-block V-8 displaced 327ci and produced 220hp. Air conditioning, mounted above the engine's right bank, was becoming an increasingly popular accessory.

the V-6 forced GMC to add an inline six obtained from Chevrolet.

1965-1966 GMCs

No styling changes occurred for 1965-66 GMCs. GMC light trucks were identical to Chevy models except for continuation of the V-6 engine.

By 1966 the typical pickup truck owner was no longer a man using his truck for work. Retired couples bought pickups to take their dream vacations, and families were buying pickups for all-around use. Comfortable, appealing interiors were part of the pickup's broadening sales base.

The 1966 example seen here combines the standard, narrow-window cab with a number of extra-cost features, including two-tone paint, chromed bumpers, pinstripe whitewall tires, and Custom side trim. This vehicle, owned by Rob Granger of Eustis, Florida, has optional air conditioning and power brakes.

front and rear fenders. On the CST models, a brightmetal band now outlined the grille area, wrapping down along the fender crests outside the headlights. A second trim strip on the side, located just below the top of the front fenders, extended the length of the truck. During both 1967 and 1968, the Chevrolet lettering appeared on the front of the hood with a red bow-tie emblem mounted in the center of the grille. The red bow tie also accompanied the series designation marker that appeared at the rear of the front fenders. As in previous years, the inscriptions C-10, C-20, and C-30 designated the light-duty models.

Although it's easy to tell a 1967 model from a 1968 by the presence or absence of the side marker lights, trucks using the small, standard hubcap were also distinguished by a more subtle difference. For 1967 the small hubcap was painted white with the bow tie in the center painted red

and surrounded by a black ring. For 1968 the small hubcap's outer ring was painted red instead of black. For both years the full hubcap available as an accessory had a large, black center inset with a red bow tie in the middle and five simulated nuts spaced in the brightmetal outer circle. The simulated lug nuts fooled a few service station trainees who thought they could remove a wheel by spinning them off with an air wrench, instead of removing the hubcap and loosening the real lug nuts. That's the main reason you sometimes see these fancy wheel covers with one or more of the decorative nuts missing.

Transmission options in the early years of this series included a manual three-speed, or a manual three-speed and overdrive (with the half-ton only); a manual four-speed; and two automatics—Chevy's Powerglide and GM's Turbo Hydra-matic. Although reliable and inexpensive to buy and repair, Powerglide offered

Although the underhood air-conditioning equipment seems compactly packaged, restorers who have converted a non-air-conditioned truck to the factory setup describe the changeover as "very challenging."

only two forward gear ratios, so the engine raced climbing out of low and slammed into drive—not a very pleasant driving sensation. For smoothness in clutch-free driving, buyers went with the Turbo Hydra-matic.

At the outset of this series, four engines were available: the base 250ci six; the larger, more powerful 292 six; and either the 283ci or the 327ci version of Chevy's popular small-block V-8. Emission controls beyond a simple positive crankcase ventilation valve hadn't yet emerged, so looking under the hood of these trucks gives a welcome sight of the engine and accessories uncluttered by pollution con-

Chevrolet pulled out all the stops with its Super Cheyenne series pickup. Note the air conditioning duct set just outside the dash panel. Built-in factory air-conditioning is a very desirable feature in these trucks.

trol accessories. These add-ons would appear before the end of the series, however.

Although currently eclipsed in collector interest by the 1969-72 models, the 1967 and 1968 Chevy light trucks were handsome in their own right and offered special options, such as overdrive, not found on the later models.

1969 Chevrolets

Executing the small styling change from a sloping hood front to a nearly ver-

tical front hood edge, plus extending a brightmetal divider across an otherwise open grille and moving the bow-tie emblem above the grille, gave Chevrolet's 1969 models a strikingly different appearance. On the CST models, a wider trim belt, gussied up with a wood-grained inset, accented the side crease, but didn't follow the wheel arch as had been the case in 1967 and 1968. All 1969-and-later trucks in this series used a two-, rather than three-, spoke steering wheel.

Along with these appearance differences, Chevrolet also introduced two new light-truck models. One of these, the instantly popular Blazer, remains in production today. The other, an elongated Fleetside called the Longhorn, was designed to carry an extra large pickup camper. Both

new models represented marketing firsts. Chevrolet's engineers created the Blazer by making the cab and box of a short-box Fleetside pickup into a single unit, and the Longhorn was a long-box Fleetside stretched 6in.

Since it used standard pickup components throughout, the Blazer had a substantially wider body and track than the Ford Bronco or International Scout, its closest competition. The familiar styling and greater comfort of a full-width truck placed the Blazer almost immediately at the top of the utility 4x4 sales charts. Of course, using standard pickup assemblies also saved GM a bundle in tooling and parts inventory.

By the late sixties, Americans were buying pickups in record numbers. Although the pickup's greater comfort accounted for a part of these sales, another reason was the number of pickups being bought for recreational use, specifically for traveling with a camper unit. It was for this recreation market that Chevrolet designed its Longhorn. With its 8 1/2ft bed, the Longhorn pickup could carry the roomiest of campers, and with a load rating of three-quarters ton or one ton, it proved easily capable of handling an oversized camper's weight. As with the Blazer, Chevy built the Longhorn using existing stampings. In this case, the extra 6in in box length were gained by adding 1/2ft-long inserts between the front of the side panels and the header. Since the inserts were placed at the front of the bed, the wheelwells were moved back 6in and required that the frame and the drive shaft be lengthened as well. All Longhorns were fitted with leaf springs in the rear. Buyers could option a Longhorn with any trim package.

In 1969 Chevrolet also expanded the interior options. Between the standard and CST interiors, a new medium-range trim package called the Custom Comfort and Appearance option became available. The popular Custom package included bright moldings around the windshield, rear window, and vent panes; a vinyl floor mat color keyed to the seat covering; embossed door panels; insulation at the cowl to quiet engine noise; and Custom nameplates on the front fenders and the glovebox door.

Also offered was a deluxe instrument panel that added individual gauges for the alternator amp reading, oil pressure, and engine temperature, at the bottom of the instrument cluster. A fourth instrument cutout in this row could hold an optional clock. Formerly, the amp reading, oil pressure, and engine temperature had been displayed as warning lights in the right-hand gauge housing. An optional tachometer could also be housed in the center gauge cutout above the steering post. The tachometer is a desirable accessory, and dash units containing a tach are hot items at flea markets.

1970 Chevrolets

It takes a fairly sharp eye to distinguish between a 1969 and a 1970 model Chevy pickup. The difference is in the grille. In 1970 a black plastic grille in a rib pattern sat behind the aluminum crosspiece. The other notable change addressed the ex-

panding pickup camper market: an optional 402ci V-8, called the 400, joined the engine line-up. This big-inch engine offered plenty of torque for towing a boat or other recreational vehicle, or hauling an extra large pickup camper.

1971 Chevrolets

To update its light-truck line for 1971, Chevy once again applied the simple but effective egg-crate grille—and created a winner. The second feature that distinguished 1971 and 1972 Chevy trucks could be seen in the optional two-toned paint scheme applied to Cheyenne and other deluxe models. Previously, two-toning limited the contrasting color—white—to the roof only. Now the contrasting color could also be applied between the trim moldings on the sides of the cab and the Fleetside bed, and across the tailgate.

A new dress-up trim and interior package called Cheyenne put Chevrolet's trucks on a solid par with a car in terms of comfort and appearance. Along with attractive outside trim that included simulated wood and brightmetal moldings along the sides of the truck and across the tailgate, the Cheyenne package gave the interior an even more comfortable look with embossed vinyl–covered seats, door panels, and headliner. The growing interest in upscale trucks could be traced to two trends: the continuing camper craze and buyers who didn't need a truck for business but wanted a pickup for its versatility. Travelers sought greater luxury for the obvious reason that if they were going to spend several weeks or months on the road toting their "home" in the pickup box, they wanted their surroundings to be comfortable and pleasant looking.

The increased emphasis on styling and interior comfort didn't mean Chevrolet was forgetting those who took their trucks to work. Among the practical options was a sliding-back window that gave flow-through cab ventilation for comfortable driving without air conditioning in warm weather. Buyers of Fleetside models could also option a lockable storage compartment that installed just ahead of the right wheelhousing. This storage locker, which measured 7x28x17in, made a handy place to carry tools and other small items like a length of rope for tying down a load. Whereas the sliding window is seen quite commonly, often as an aftermarket replacement, the storage compartment is quite rare.

Appearance aside, the most significant improvement in Chevy's 1971 light trucks came in the form of front disc brakes. Almost anyone who has driven both a drum brake truck and a disc brake truck immediately appreciates the quicker braking response and greater stopping power of front disc brakes. Other mechanical changes were also occurring, but without fanfare. As the auto manufacturers struggled to meet tightening governmental air quality regulations, engines became encumbered with air pumps, compression ratios decreased, and power output slackened. Trucks built for sale in California had to meet stiffer requirements and were equipped with air pumps—which fed fresh air into the exhaust manifold to reduce nitrous oxides and carbon monoxide—as early as 1969. The antipollution equipment had two noticeable effects: engine performance declined, as did gasoline mileage.

1972 Chevrolets

The most visible differences between the 1971 and 1972 models occurred in the trim packages. A new interior decor, consisting of cloth seat inserts in a Scots plaid pattern, was marketed under the Highlander name and identified by Highlander nameplates under the series marker on the front fenders. The plaid seat inserts came in four color patterns—blue, gray, avocado, and orange—to match the various exterior colors.

A Super Cheyenne model made its debut in 1972. This trim package also featured cloth seat inserts, though in a houndstooth pattern. Other features of this package included a chromed tailgate release handle and identifying nameplates on the front fenders and the glovebox door. Reflecting the shift in interest from pickup campers to motor homes, the Longhorn bowed out in 1971.

The Chevrolet Blazer

For sixteen years, from 1945 to 1961, the Jeep had enjoyed the utility four-wheel-drive market virtually to itself. In 1961 International entered the small but potentially lucrative utility 4x4 market with its versatile Scout. In 1966 Ford went after its slice of the growing market for go-anywhere vehicles with the Bronco. Both the Scout and the Bronco were larger than the Jeep but smaller than a standard pickup. By designing the Blazer to pickup proportions, Chevrolet offered the first utility 4x4 that would comfortably seat a family—precisely what the market wanted.

In popular CST form, the Blazer came equipped with a fully carpeted floor, including the cargo area; front bucket seats with a lidded fiberglass storage box as a seat divider and a two-person bench seat perched on the cargo floor; a removable fiberglass hardtop; vinyl trim panels in the doors and along the insides of the box; and decorative exterior trim. It made a very appealing package. With the rear seat removed and the tailgate down, the cargo area extended 8ft—ideal for hauling building supplies. In this sense the Blazer was really a shortened pickup, and to prove the point, it was also available in two-wheel drive with front coil springs, though few examples of this configuration were sold.

The removable convertible hardtop feature added to the Blazer's sales appeal. Lifting off the fiberglass top was not a simple five-minute job, however. The top clamped to the windshield header and bolted to the body along the tops of the rear side panels. Instructions in the owner's manual warned that before removing the top, a cradle had to be built to keep the top from collapsing when lifted off the vehicle. Otherwise, the weight of the rear glass windows would cause the roof to bow, cracking the fiberglass. Fortunately, few owners removed the tops from their vehicles and collectors report little problem with damage to the fiberglass.

The Chevrolet Carryall Suburban

Chevrolet's Carryall Suburban continued to be one of the most versatile vehicles for hauling the maximum number of passengers, plus cargo, whether on-road or off. With four-wheel drive, the Suburban ensured safe travel regardless of road condition and could bushwhack a group of hunters into camp. For strictly highway travel, the riding qualities of the two-wheel-drive version with coil spring IFS matched those of a large station wagon. In either drivetrain configuration, the Suburban made an ideal vehicle for towing a sizable travel trailer. Auxiliary rear leaf springs and engine options to 400ci gave the Suburban a truck's pulling power. For

large families, schools, farmers, hunters, mineral exploration companies, and vacation-bound travelers, the Suburban matched truck strength with better-than-station wagon roominess and packaged this combination in Chevy's attractive truck styling

The Chevrolet Panel

With a floor load length of 116in, 1967-72 panel trucks had truly spacious cargo capacity and today make ideal tow rigs and parts haulers for serious old-car and -truck collectors. As with the Suburban, panels were built on both the C-10 (half-ton) and C-20 (three-quarter-ton) chassis and could be found with Chevrolet's full range of engine options. Most panel trucks were supplied in rather plain-Jane fashion, with a single seat for the driver and the lowest level of trim and interior decor. However, all the optional dress-up equipment available on a Suburban could also be specified on a panel truck, though seating options were limited to a companion bucket seat on the passenger's side.

GMCs

Differences between Chevrolet and GMC light trucks had now become superficial, extending primarily to the grille, which throughout the 1967-72 series consisted of a crossbar design, and nameplates. GMC introduced its version of the Blazer, called the Jimmy, in 1970—a model year later than Chevrolet. Along with the Jimmy, GMC also built its version of the Longhorn, but without any distinguishing nameplates.

Fleetside shortbox models, particularly from the Cheyenne series that was available only in 1971 and 1972, are probably the most desirable of all Chevrolet trucks, Cameo models excluded. In 1971, all Chevrolet full-size pickups were equipped with front disk brakes, which dramatically improved stopping ability. On the C-10 models, coil spring suspension front and rear resulted in a boulevard-smooth ride, even on unpaved surfaces. Other comfort features included optional bucket seats and air conditioning. The truck shown here is a 1972 model.

Chevrolet's new truck styling for 1973 featured rounded lines and a very low roof profile. Up-class models, such as the Scottsdale shown here, offered handsome two-toned paint schemes with the contrasting color set off with bright trim. Chevrolet Division, General Motors Corporation

Chapter 9

Rounded-Line Models, 1973-1987

With collectors swarming around the 1967-72 styling series trucks, the 1973-88 models have largely gone overlooked, except as they continue to fulfill their role as working vehicles. With the exception of the potentially hazardous location of the fuel tank outside the frame rails, these modern-era full-sized trucks represent dependable engineering and many comfort advances over their predecessors.

The most prominent styling feature of this series of Chevrolet trucks is their rounded lines, particularly visible in the windshield contour and door window outlines. Rounded lines are also prominent in the curvature at the tops of the doors and the rear box corners. With the top of the doors actually cutting into the roof, this series showed almost no roof height. The high door cutout helped entry and exit, but also caused problems on early trucks, as the doors curved in at the top, and since rain gutters had been eliminated to give a smoother look, riding with the windows down in even a light rain resulted in water running off the roof and into the cab. To prevent this irritation, Chevrolet dealers sold bright plastic rain gutters that could be attached to the edge of the roof above the doors with sheet metal screws. Buyers protested, and soon Chevy made roof gutters a standard feature.

With the introduction of the new styling series, two changes occurred in Chevrolet's light-truck line-up: the popular, spacious vans had finally made panel trucks obsolete, and a six-passenger, four-door Crew Cab pickup was now available on either the C-20 chassis or the C-30 chassis. On the C-30 chassis, the Crew Cab pickup could be ordered with dual wheels in combination with the Camper Special option package. As any pickup camper owner probably knows, the high, heavy camper unit can cause a truck to rock uncomfortably in strong winds and on rough roads. Dual rear wheels reduced this rocking motion and gave more stability to the top-heavy camper load.

Besides rear leaf springs, changes to the chassis included finned rear brake drums and an energy-absorbing steering column, which was designed to collapse upon impact. The high-torque 250 six remained the base engine. In C-20 and C-30 models, the larger 292 six could be optioned, along with the 350 and 454 V-8s. Through several years of this series, the 305 and 400 V-8s were also available. The 400ci V-8, which Chevrolet also used in its mid-seventies, was a small-block–based engine. The 454 descended from Chevrolet's big-block series engines. In 1978, to counter the fall in fuel economy that had resulted from engines being detuned to meet clean air standards, Chevy offered a 5.7-liter V-8 diesel, based on its 350 V-8 gasoline engine, in the C-10 models only. A larger, 6.2-liter (379ci displacement) diesel became available for the heavier-duty models in 1982. No other light-truck manufacturer even came close to matching Chevrolet's range of engine offerings.

In keeping with the trend toward more upscale trucks, Chevrolet now offered four exterior trim and interior comfort packages. The Custom package, which had been a midline offering in the previous series, now became the base appearance and comfort model. A Custom truck's interior color coordinated the padded dash covering, seat upholstery, and door panels with the paint finish. The rubber floor mat, however, was black. The seat upholstery consisted of vinyl bolsters and color-coordinated fabric inserts. Dual sun visors and a roof panel all painted to match the truck's exterior completed the interior appointments. The exterior, with its painted bumper and hubcaps and absence of bright windshield or rear window trim, identified a working truck—despite the Custom nameplates.

Moving up, buyers could opt for the Cheyenne comfort and trim package that had been top-of-the-line in the previous series. Here, extra insulation produced a quieter cab and the interior presented a richer vinyl or nylon cloth seat covering, storage pockets in the doors, and color-coordinated nylon carpeting. A chromed front bumper and hubcaps, bright trim around the marker lights and brightmetal moldings on the tailgate of Fleetside mod-

When Chevrolet's New Era trucks first appeared, it looked as though the stepside model had disappeared from the line-up. However, the ever-popular narrow-box pickup quickly returned, though now with the rear fenders molded into the sides of the box. Four Wheeler magazine selected the 4x4 Sportside, as the narrow-box model was now called, as its Four Wheeler of the Year for 1988. Chevrolet Division, General Motors Corporation

els, plus Cheyenne nameplates identified this dress-up model.

Above the Cheyenne, the Cheyenne Super comfort and trim package added extra thick seat padding plus herringbone-striped nylon cloth or special vinyl seat coverings, a wood-grained instrument panel with full instrumentation, and an insulated headliner to the standard Cheyenne features. Bucket seats with a center console could be optioned in place of the bench seat. Outside markings included brightmetal wheel opening moldings and the Cheyenne Super nameplate—as well as all other Cheyenne trim.

Whereas the instrument panels of previous Chevy trucks were businesslike in both appearance and function, the gauge layout and instrument panel design now resembled that found on an upscale touring sedan like the Pontiac Grand Prix. The

instrument clusters on the top-of-the-line trim models, with their wood-grained or brush-finished stainless steel panels, presented an outright luxury image. The easy-to-see gauge layout placed the speedometer and optional tachometer or clock in the center of the panel in front of the driver, with smaller gauges for fuel, amps, oil pressure, and temperature—or a combination of gauges and warning lights—on an angled panel to the left. Another angled panel to the right of the main gauge cluster contained the heater–air conditioning and radio controls—when these accessories were optioned. Now the driver could turn on the defroster or select a different radio station without having to lean away from the steering wheel and reach over to the center of the dash. The new dash layout grouped all controls directly in front of the driver.

Along with the posh interiors and improved instrument cluster design, Chevy trucks now incorporated several comfort features found formerly only on cars. These included a tilt steering wheel, cruise control, side mirrors mounted at the beltline so as not to obstruct forward vision, and an AM/FM radio with the antenna molded into the windshield. Other comfort extras, including power steering, power brakes, air conditioning, and bucket seats carried over from the previous series. The new pickups also offered a sliding rear

window, which not only greatly improved cab comfort on non-air-conditioned trucks during hot weather driving, but also improved heater and air conditioning performance. Later in this series, Chevrolet added tinted glass as well as power windows and door latches to the list of comfort and convenience features.

Early Blazers in this series had the fully removable fiberglass cap. In 1976, out of concern for driver and passenger safety in the event of a rollover, Chevrolet redesigned the Blazer so that a metal cab covered the front seats. A removable fiberglass cap could be installed to enclose either the rear seat or cargo area, or both. With the cap in place, the only noticeable difference between the earlier and later Blazers—apart from different grilles and other styling changes—was the seam where the cap joined the cab. There was, of course, a big difference in the early and later models when the caps were removed. Taking off the cap made a 1973-75 Blazer into a full convertible, whereas on a 1976 or later Blazer, lifting off the cap exposed the cargo area and gave rear seat passengers a fresh air ride. Since most Blazers came equipped with the removable cap, there appears to be an adequate supply of these caps.

Chevrolet offered four-wheel drive on its Suburban also, though the two-wheel-drive version of this jumbo station wagon

continued to be more popular. Although competitors have put models up against the Suburban—most notably the International Travelall and the Dodge Carryall—Chevy has found a strong market for this truck-car hybrid that it continues to grow. In the previous styling series, Suburbans had been equipped with three side doors—one for the driver and two on the passenger's side. This arrangement, though perhaps safer for loading and unloading at curbside, proved awkward for second- and third-seat passengers, so the redesigned Suburban now had four side doors.

Besides changes to the grille—which consisted mainly of variations on the grid theme—the general styling of Chevrolet's light trucks remained the same from 1973 to 1980. Considering that the previous styling series had gone six years, a seven-year stretch was a long time to keep the same truck before the public. In 1981 Chevrolet executed a quite simple but attractive facelift by giving a slight slope to the hood, bringing the side crease to a point just behind the grille, and making the front of the truck essentially flat, as opposed to the previous grille's forward thrust. The grille now enclosed quad headlights and featured a bright horizontal bar that bore a resemblance to the center dividing bar on Chevy's 1969 and 1970 trucks. For 1981-83 models, the

parking lights were moved to the bumper, as in 1971-72.

Although Chevy trucks in this styling series have a strong reputation for dependability and service, their safety has been called into question by deaths that have resulted from fires caused by collision impacts that have ruptured the side-mounted fuel tank. While collectors have typically not put safety high among their reasons for preferring one truck model over another, the fuel tank location is a factor to consider when contemplating the purchase of a Chevrolet or GMC truck from this styling series.

GMCs

About the only distinguishing differences of GMC trucks of the 1973-87 styling series were the GMC emblems and nameplates, and grilles that used a more open grid pattern than Chevrolet's. Mechanically and in sheet metal, GMC trucks in this styling series were entirely Chevrolet. GMC called its version of Chevy's Cheyenne the Sierra Grande, and the Blazer under GMC badges became the Jimmy. A GMC model that would make nearly a unique collector truck was the Jimmy Casa Grande. This was a special 1976 model that consisted of a very compact camper body mounted on the short Jimmy pickup box and tied into the metal cab. A pop-up

The unquestioned king of the New Era line-up was Chevrolet's SS 454 muscle pickup. Dressed all in black with red SS 454 lettering on the box sides, this high-stepping truck easily intimidated the competition. For 1990 Chevrolet held production to one for each dealer, making the SS 454 an instant collector truck. Chevrolet Division, General Motors Corporation

top on the camper body, when expanded, gave a headroom height of 6ft, 7in. The cab's open rear gave easy access to the camper, which was designed to sleep two—with an optional overhead bunk for sleeping four—and was equipped with a liquefied petroleum gas stove and refrigerator. However, the camper's compact space didn't allow room for shower or bathroom facilities. GMC also built a distinctive, low-production pickup truck called the Gentleman Jim, which was easily distinguished by its black-and-silver paint scheme and decals on the rear flanks of the pickup box.

Although many buyers continued to regard GMC as an upscale Chevrolet, the real difference between the two names was buyer preference. Except among those to whom the GMC nameplate means something special, the Chevrolet name typically commands greater collector appeal.

Chevrolet's latest generation of full-sized pickups has evolved into trucks like this 1994 K1500 Sportside, with its design reminiscent of the classic stepside styling. This particular model has four-wheel drive and, like all modern pickups, a cab whose interior is as plush and well-appointed as practically any car of its era. Chevrolet Division, General Motors Corporation

Chapter 10

Full-Sized Models, 1988-1994

Truck buyers tend to be on the conservative side and shy away from big, bold changes. Yet bold, sweeping changes are what truck buyers saw when they entered Chevrolet showrooms in the spring of 1988 to eye the all-new line-up of Chevy full-sized pickups and Blazers. Besides the rounded styling, sharply raked windshield profile, and flush-mounted window glass, the most noticeable feature of the New Era trucks was the slimmer profile. The narrower width meant a slight decrease in the overall size of the Fleetside box, but cleverly designed indents in the box sidewalls allowed the placing of cross-braces to support a double-tiered load. The double-deck load arrangement actually resulted in a more efficient use of the cargo space and a greater load capacity, particularly for carrying building supplies.

The cross-brace idea was just one of numerous features that made these Chevy trucks more pleasurable to own and operate. For years pickup owners were plagued with an underbox location for the spare tire. If a tire failed on the road, you had to crawl under the box, mash your knuckles trying to loosen the spare carrier's retaining nut, which usually had become rust frozen from moisture or road salt, then wrestle the spare off the carrier. When placing the spare back on the carrier, you had to support the weight of the tire and the carrier while rethreading the retaining nut. It was a brute force job, guaranteed to make you look as if you'd spent a half day underneath a vehicle. With all the hassle the underbox spare tire created, many owners threw out the carrier and toted the spare inside the box—where it got in the way of cargo and invited theft. The underbox spare didn't make friends with female pickup owners and drivers either. So how did Chevy solve the spare tire storage problem? By devising a crank-down mechanism that used a ratchet handle inserted through a hole in the rear bumper to lower the tire quickly and easily onto the pavement. Does anyone remember where the idea for a crank-down spare tire originated? That's right, Chevy's imported LUV pickup.

Another handy benefit of Chevy's full-sized New Era trucks was a storage platform behind the front seat for tools or an attache case. The storage area wasn't large, but it was ideal for items that formerly would have been placed on the floor or on the seat—and be a nuisance in either location. Although not a new feature, the tailgate was removed easily by unlatching the supports and lifting the gate off its pivots. The removable tailgate had advantages for distance travel—an upright gate acts as an air dam at interstate speeds—and some loads were carried more easily with the tailgate removed.

Unquestionably, Chevy New Era trucks have strong styling appeal. The wind-sweep shape made a complete departure from the bulky lines of the past, yet designers were careful to maintain the Chevrolet identity through the full-width split grille. Styling Chevrolet's trucks for the nineties brought many challenges, not the least of which was automating a large proportion of the manufacture and assembly processes. Robots were used extensively for welding and painting, and computers were instrumental in the design and testing of most components. Advanced technology could be found inside the truck as well as in its construction. Fuel was metered to the engine by electronic fuel injection. Computers sensed and prevented rear brake lockup for safe, fast stops. Four-wheel-drive models featured Insta-Trac shifting, which let the driver select two- or four-wheel drive at any speed. Instrument readings were displayed with high-tech, bar graph–style gauges. And as would be expected at the brink of the twenty-first century, Chevy New Era trucks were engineered for driving and riding comfort through such details as wide, easy-access doors that reached upward into the roofline; low step-in height; high headroom; and extra legroom and footroom inside the cab. Even the seats were high-tech, not just in manufacture, but in being better suited to the human form for more comfortable, long-distance driving. All the convenience and comfort features associated with cars were also found in Chevy's New Era trucks—from tilt steering

It will be a few years before modern trucks such as this 1993 K1500 regular cab longbox with four-wheel-drive is considered collectible. But you can bet that when a few decades pass and collectors zero in on trucks of the eighties and nineties, they'll pay special attention to models loaded with features such as those shown here: original multi-color paint, side moldings, four-wheel-drive, optional cast aluminum wheels, large side mirrors, sliding window at the rear of the cab, bucket seats, and an interior loaded with luxury appointments. Chevrolet Division, General Motors Corporation

to cruise control, power windows, power locks, and sophisticated sound systems, whether radio only or radio and cassette tape player.

When the New Era trucks appeared in 1988, it looked as though the stepside model had disappeared from the line-up. One could argue, perhaps, that the narrow box, which traced back to the original pickup trucks, had become obsolete. But the narrow box gives a pickup a classic look, and to their great credit, Chevy stylists undertook to preserve the narrow box while giving it a modern look. They did this by creating wedge-shaped fenders that were molded into the fiberglass box sides, placing the taillights at the ends of the box, as on the Fleetside, and by molding steps both fore and aft of the rear fenders, into the box sides. Below the steps the box contour followed the lower bodyline of the cab. Far from being the basic bread-and-butter truck, Chevy's classic stepside pickup was now a work-and-

play model, appropriately named Sport-side.

Among the features that gave the New Era Chevy trucks their ultramodern look was the flush-mounted windows. The flush-mounted glass resulted in a more streamlined appearance and put Chevy's trucks in the same league with cars that used this advanced glass-mounting technology. Also new to Chevy's full-sized truck line was the extended cab pickup. In its S-10 compact-pickup line, Chevy had marketed Maxi-cab trucks since 1983. Chevy's full-sized extended cab pickups featured a fold-down, full-width rear bench seat. Since the back of the extended cab had no downward slope, rear seat passengers had full headroom. With the rear seat folded up, the extended cab afforded nearly 40cu-ft of storage space for gear or luggage.

In 1990 Chevrolet entered the performance truck arena with a special SS 454 sport pickup. Equipped with the Fleetside short box and 7.4-liter (454ci) heavy-duty engine, plus a performance handling package and locking rear axle, the SS 454 came in one color combination: Chevrolet's racing black with black painted trim. There's no mistaking the SS 454 for other than what it was: a high-image muscle truck. The SS 454 decals on the rear flanks gave this special pickup instant recognition. In front, the all-black grille was punctuated with a red-outlined Chevy bow-tie emblem and carried halogen composite headlights. Inside, the SS 454 was dressed with the Silverado trim decor consisting of

high-backed sport bucket seats and a center console. An appealing, high-contrast Garnet red interior color scheme was selected for this special truck. As a top-of-the-line model, the SS 454 came standard equipped with deluxe comfort, convenience, and sound packages.

Chevrolet also expanded its Blazer line from two models—the full-sized Blazer and the junior S Blazer based on the S-10 truck line—to three with a four-door S model. This truck, which Chevrolet described as the "wagon of the '90s," was one of the most handsome models in Chevrolet's New Era truck line-up. Besides the two additional doors, which gave much easier access to the rear seat compartment, the four-door Blazer also provided an added 7 1/2in of space behind the front seats—giving more legroom to rear seat passengers and expanding cargo space when the rear seat was folded down. Interiors of the four-door S Blazer, along with those of other Blazer models, were every bit as luxurious as the interiors of a car, with full carpeting; rich, leather-appearing vinyl or deluxe cloth seat coverings and matching door trim; an overhead lighting console; and a comfortable, leather-wrapped steering wheel.

The four-door companion to the full-sized Blazer was, of course, Chevrolet's popular Suburban, which was available in two-wheel drive or Insta-Trac four-wheel drive. Besides its spacious size—allowing comfortable seating for up to nine passengers—this queen of Chevrolet's light-truck fleet also offered unmatched towing ca-

pacity for pulling travel or horse trailers, boats, or other sport or hobby equipment. As with the New Era Blazer, the four-wheel-drive Suburban featured a torsion bar IFS for ride smoothness equal to that of a car. Besides giving the Blazer and the Suburban the ability to glide over bumps and rough pavement, IFS offered the benefit of lowering step-up height to the vehicle without sacrificing ground clearance. In comparison with previous Blazers and Suburbans, the New Era models had a much lower and sleeker profile for reduced wind resistance and fuel economy, without sacrificing interior space.

The pattern that has evolved in the automotive industry is that as new levels of interior and exterior trim are introduced, the names for the former top-of-the-line packages migrate downward. This pattern was certainly visible in Chevrolet's New Era trucks, where the base interior and trim package was now called Cheyenne. As would be expected on a working vehicle, the Cheyenne exterior was devoid of brightwork or side moldings, whereas inside, the Cheyenne trucks were upholstered in a durable yet not unattractive vinyl. Still built to work, but also dressed in elegance, Chevy full-sized trucks wearing the Silverado package were distinguished by bright-accented wheel openings; an aluminum applique containing Chevrolet lettering on the tailgate; swing-out side windows on extended cab models; and a brightmetal outline around the grille, side moldings, and chrome front bumper. In-

side, the Silverado package provided a custom vinyl seat with a folding center armrest, or cloth-covered seats at no extra cost; color-keyed carpeting; removable front floor mats; two-toned door trim; a full cloth headliner; and cloth-covered sun visors.

S-10 personal-sized pickups also came in two trim packages. The standard gave a work truck look and feel with painted bumpers and grille surround and a vinyl interior. The Tahoe dress-up package with its chrome grille and smart side trim, plus upscale cloth or vinyl interior, outfitted an S-10 for any setting.

Powertrain packages for the New Era full-sized and personal-sized trucks were designed for maximum power and fuel economy. Standard engines in the 1500 and 2500 series full-sized pickups included GM's 4.3-liter (262ci) Vortex V-6. The venerable 5.7-liter (350ci) V-8 was optional or standard in 3500 series full-sized trucks as well as Blazers and Suburbans, and a 6.5-liter (396ci) turbo diesel V-8 was optional in all series pickups. Both transmission options—a five-speed manual or a four-speed automatic—featured built-in overdrive gearing. The S-10 offered a fuel-frugal 2.5-liter L4 as its base engine, with a 2.8-liter V-6 or the gutsy 4.3-liter Vortex V-6 as an option; the Vortex came standard in Insta-Trac 4x4 models.

After wearing the sales crown for decades, Chevy trucks slipped behind Fords in a fiercely fought sales battle in 1992, and fell off more sharply in 1993—owing per-

This 1993 C2500 full-size pickup looks pretty plain, but its rarity may help its eventual collectability. Engine options for the 2500 series included larger-displacement high-performance engines that result in these trucks having greater payload and towing capacities than 1500 series trucks. Chevrolet Division, General Motors Corporation

haps to GM's corporate image problems in those years. However, this sales decline did not reflect on the quality or styling of Chevrolet New Era trucks, which continued to be leading edge in the light-truck field. Chevrolet trucks have inspired a loyalty unmatched by that of any other make, and this loyalty continued in a decade when brand allegiance meant next to nothing to new-car buyers. And perhaps most telling of all, Chevrolet trucks could boast an unmatched reputation for durability, with 98 percent of all Chevrolet full-sized pickups built in the preceding ten years still on the road in 1994. From a durability and brand loyalty standpoint, Chevrolet was still the king.

GMCs

Today's GMC trucks are clones of Chevrolet versions, marketed with the GMC nameplate and different model names. As with the compact S-15 line, GMC called its extended cab full-sized truck the Club Coupe. Blazers in the GMC family were Jimmys, and full-sized pickups belonged to the Sierra group.

Chevrolet's compact pickup offerings have evolved from the old LUV to this, the 1994 S-10 pickup. Just like the full-sized trucks, it is available in several models and with several different performance and accessory packages. Shown here, in fact, is an S-10 with the four-wheel drive ZR2 Performance Package, which permits the truck to drive right out of the showroom and into off-road use. Chevrolet Division, General Motors Corporation

Chapter 11

LUV and S-10, 1972-1994

The Chevrolet LUV

In 1972 GM teamed up with Japan's Isuzu Motors to introduce the compact Chevy LUV pickup to the US market. No attempt was made to style the LUV as a downsized Chevy truck; rather, the small pickup closely resembled similar offerings from other Japanese manufacturers, notably Toyota and Nissan. The LUV's virtues were its low price, starting at $2,196 on the 1972 model; good fuel economy; good riding qualities thanks to IFS; and a 1190lb payload rating. The four-cylinder overhead cam engine displaced 110.8ci and developed 75hp. A four-speed, fully synchronized manual transmission with shift lever on the floor gave a versatile power range for all types of driving, from working off the road to cruising down the interstate.

Although the LUV carried the Chevrolet nameplate and bow-tie emblem, and could be serviced at Chevrolet garages, no attempt was made to disguise its import origins, until the restyling of 1981. At that point, oddly enough, Chevy was about ready to introduce its own, US-built compact trucks, which by 1983 would replace the LUV entirely in the Chevrolet line-up.

Japanese-built cars and trucks of the sixties and seventies made an interesting contrast with their American counterparts. First, there are the subtle extras that showed the designer's concern for the owner. On the LUV, these extras included a stowage area behind the seat for tools, packages, an attache case, or compact luggage; tie-down hooks on the sides and ends of the box; and a crank-down spare tire that was lowered mechanically from its storage area under the bed—no crawling under the truck and wrestling with a latch and tire carrier on these trucks. Although everyone appreciates convenience features such as these, not everyone has a taste for the oriental styling touches of LUV-vintage Japanese vehicles. For example, the striped Mikado upholstery of 1975 could make you feel as if you'd strayed into a rug shop in an oriental bazaar. Then there are the oval instrument clusters that stare out from the dash like a pair of cat's eyes.

As would be expected with a downsized truck, box dimensions were quite small. The box length measured 6ft, which meant lowering the tailgate to carry standard 8ft-long building supplies. The box width, measuring just over 39in between the wheelwells, posed a bigger problem when toting home wallboard or 4x8ft sheets of plywood. The solution was to lay wide items across the tops of the wheelwells. In 1978 a longer, 7 1/2ft box became available as an option. Chevrolet advertised this box as the longest of any economy-sized pickup. The load rating of the long-box LUV increased to 1650lb.

Owners of LUV trucks felt that they got good value, and the Isuzu import gave Chevrolet an economy pickup until it developed its own US-built small-truck line.

The Chevrolet S-10

Chevy introduced its home-built downsized pickup in the fall of 1981. To build the S-10, GM renovated its Dayton, Ohio, assembly plant and modernized the assembly line with robotics to ensure high quality standards and improve efficiency. Although the S-10 had a GM family look, we can now see that its styling presaged that of the new full-sized truck line to be introduced in 1988, rather than resembling the big-truck styling of the time, which was looking dated—and rightfully so, since it had already been around for nine years. Chevy dealers continued to sell LUV pickups through 1982, and since both small trucks with the Chevrolet nameplates now looked like first cousins, if not twins—the LUV's new styling of 1981 had more rounded lines, whereas the S-10's shape could best be described as angular—one might wonder on just what basis a Chevy salesperson would have urged buyers toward one over the other, apart from the S-10's Made in USA label.

Like the LUV, the S-10 came standard with a four-cylinder engine. The LUV engine, which featured an overhead camshaft, produced 80hp from a displacement of 110.8ci. The standard four-cylinder S-10 engine had a traditional pushrod overhead valve design and put out 82hp

'75 CHEVY LUV PICKUP

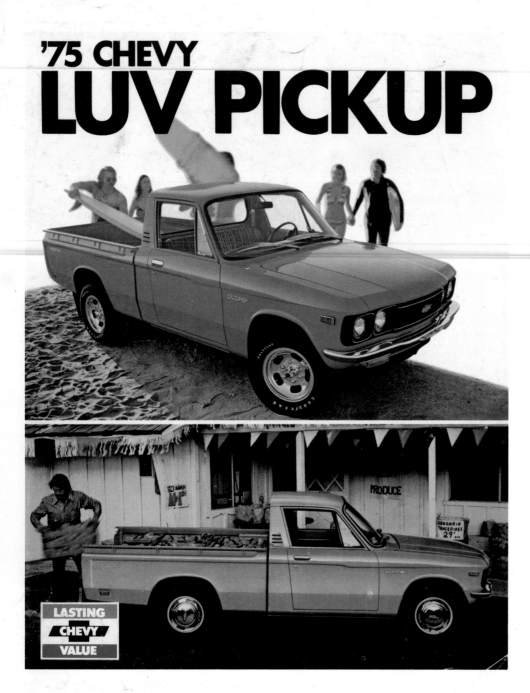

LASTING CHEVY VALUE

From 1972 until 1981, when GM introduced its own compact pickup, Chevrolet dealers sold a mini pickup called the Chevy LUV, which was built in Japan by Isuzu Motors. This well-built, reliable truck featured such engineering advances as an overhead cam four-cylinder engine and a cleverly designed cranking mechanism for stowing the spare tire under the box.

from 119ci. Surely no salesperson could build a case on a 2hp edge, and the larger displacement of the S-10 engine indicated a less efficient design. The S-10's power edge came from an optional V-6,

which for 1982 produced 110hp from 173ci. Here the salesperson had something to talk about.

The new S-10 pickups also had a slightly longer wheelbase than the LUV—108in versus 102in. Although the bed length remained the same at 6ft, the longer wheelbase put the rear wheels slightly farther back for a less choppy ride.

Chevy's home-built compact pickups met with instant acceptance and sales success, as can be seen by calendar year 1982 production figures, which showed that Chevy sold 177,758 S-10 pickups and only 22,304 LUVs. The S-10 sales also com-

pared very favorably with those of the large pickups, which had totaled 393,277 for the same period.

In 1983 Chevrolet expanded the S-10 line with a new compact Blazer. This little, go-anywhere truck was also an instant winner. Although downsized in exterior dimensions—it measured 15.3in shorter and 14.8in narrower than its full-sized namesake—it lost only 4.8sq-ft in interior floor space. The littler Blazer's four-cylinder or V-6 engine delivered substantially better fuel economy than the powerplants of the full-sized model, and the S-10's lines adopted the Blazer configuration so well that the compact Blazer made a very handsome truck. The truck's power and the looks were both significant contributors to its sales success.

S-10 interiors also reflected changes in this pickup's origin and use. From the standard interior, with its vinyl-covered bench seat, color-coated door panels, and rubber floor mat, deluxe interiors progressed from a custom cloth or vinyl-trimmed bench seat and carpeted floor covering to handsome, comfortable bucket seats, full floor carpeting, and richer-looking door trim. Many buyers were now choosing compact pickups as second cars or for commuting, general use, and occasional light hauling. In this market a comfortable, good-looking interior ranked as important as exterior appearance or engineering features.

Small pickups had also become popular with recreational users. Besides farmers and construction outfits that needed the extra traction for off-road terrain, small pickups with four-wheel-drive appealed to hunters and those who enjoyed camping and getting out into the wilderness. Chevy had offered four-wheel drive as an option on its LUV pickup since 1979, and in 1983 extended this option to its S-10 trucks.

In 1984 Chevy offered a 2.2-liter diesel in its two-wheel-drive S-10 trucks. This option was not especially popular, but at the time, diesels were in vogue as the solution to fuel economy concerns. In more recent years, GM's 4.3-liter V-6—an engine created by cutting two cylinders off the small-block V-8—rated at 160hp, has supplemented the 2.8-liter V-6 as an optional S-10 powerplant. An inline four, now displacing 2.5 liters and rated at 94hp—up 12hp from the original S-10 four—was the standard engine as recently as 1994.

Other improvements on the original S-10 design included a long-box pickup with a box length of 89in, a Getrag-licensed five-speed manual transmission with overdrive, electronic fuel injection, antilock rear brakes, and Insta-Trac—the four-wheel-drive system that allows shifting from two- to four-wheel-drive and back at any speed.

In 1989 Chevrolet introduced an upscale S-10 model called the Cameo—reviving the name of Chevy's spectacular mid-fifties dream truck. The Cameo consisted of an appearance package that included plastic ground effects, foglights, a tailgate without the Chevrolet name stamping, and Cameo decals. These special models were available in white, red, or black single colors, and Sky Blue and Mint Green tone-on-tone colors. The Cameo appearance package was discontinued in 1991.

With the S-10 Chevrolet created a highly popular light truck that not only provided economical transport for businesses that didn't need a full-sized pickup, but also served as handsome, comfortable transportation for commuters, families, and singles. And in 4x4 form, this truck was a highly versatile recreation vehicle as well.

By the nineties the angular look of Chevy's S-10 and the GMC Sonoma pickups was dated. After all, these trucks had changed little in overall appearance since their introduction in 1981. To let the public know that new styling was on the way, the all-new 1994 GMC Sonoma pickup joined the auto show circuit early in 1993, and test drives of GM's handsomely reworked compact pickup appeared in major automotive magazines as early as the April 1993 issues. This advance publicity had two purposes: to keep Chevy and GMC compact-pickup buyers from looking too seriously at the competition, and to let small-truck shoppers in general know that new handsome-looking compact trucks wearing Chevrolet and GMC nameplates were right around the corner.

The new styling was indeed good-looking. From the forward-sloping hood and gently rounded front bumper to the flowing cab contours that blended smoothly into the pickup box to the gracefully curved tailgate and taillights set tastefully into the rear fenders, GM's small pickups were up-to-date once again. Every bit as important as styling, the new-for-'94 small trucks featured an abundance of updated technical features, including an antilock braking system (ABS), plus chassis

bracing for a smoother, quieter ride. With its 1994 S-10 and Sonoma pickups, GM regained its competitiveness in the highly wired small-truck market.

GMCs

The LUV never acquired a GMC nameplate, so throughout the seventies, buyers of GMC trucks had to be content with full-sized GMC offerings only. GM may have reasoned that the absence of a small pickup actually fit the GMC image and that a badge-engineered LUV for GMC dealers would find few buyers. If this was the thinking, the logic changed 180 degrees with GM's home-built small trucks, because GMC got its version of the Chevy S-10, rather fittingly named the S-15. Actually, the S-15 was identical to Chevy's S-10 with the exception of the grille, the nameplates, and some sport interior offerings. Both trucks came down the same assembly line, and at least one GMC salesman reported that S-15 trucks have come into their garage with Chevrolet decals on the tailgate and sides—

Chevy's own compact pickup, called the S-10, set the styling pattern for GM's New Era trucks, which would appear in 1988. Among the popular models in the S-10 line-up was the extended cab model shown here with accessories from the Back Country package that include the rugged grille guard and light bridge mounted on the head of the pickup box. Chevrolet Division, General Motors Corporation

"Pranks," he said, "by the assembly line workers."

To many buyers the GMC name still means "the Cadillac of trucks"—a compliment the GMC salesman isn't likely to dispute. From the skin inward, though, today's GMC is really a Chevrolet, or vice versa.

Chevrolet made a hybrid of its compact pickup trucks and its Blazer—the S-10 Blazer—and then restyled it so that by 1993 it had four passenger doors. It was one of the Bow Tie division's entrants in the competitive sport-utility market. Chevrolet Division, General Motors Corporation

Chapter 12

Truck in a Car Wrapper: El Camino, 1959-1987

For 1959 and 1960, GM's hardtop styling featured a very thin roof supported by narrow posts. The resulting large glass area made for excellent visibility and gave the impression that the driver and passengers were enclosed in a bubble. The El Camino received a stunted version of this hardtop styling, complete with thin roof pillars and wraparound rear as well as front window glass. All GM car lines had taken a major styling plunge in 1959 that can be called futuristic or simply bizarre, depending on your tastes. As a member of the Chevrolet family, the El Camino shared the styling idiosyncrasies of that year's Chevrolet cars: thin air scoops in the front of the hood that some say looked like eyebrows and to others resembled jet intakes, and sweeping gullwing fins at the rear.

Though they served no functional purpose, the deeply sculpted gullwing fins lent an appearance of motion, much like

With its 1959 El Camino, Chevrolet created the most outspoken, outlandish pickup design of all time. From its "cat's eye" front fender eyebrows to the gullwing fins at the rear, the 1959 El Camino looks poised to rocket off to a distant galaxy. The El Camino's pace-setting advances didn't stop with styling. Engine options included the hot 290hp, fuel-injected 283ci V-8, and the blistering 335hp 348ci big-block. With one of those engines and a four-speed transmission, an El Camino could show its taillights to practically all challengers at the Saturday night drag races.

The V insignia on this El Camino's nosepiece indicates a V-8 engine under the hood.

the extended wings of a bird or an aircraft, even when an El Camino—or any other 1959 Chevrolet car model—was standing still. The real trick for the stylists came with what to do with the audacious wings at the vehicle's tail. The El Camino's view from the rear was every bit as dramatic as the view from any other perspective. As the cut below the wings swept downward, ending in a cat's-eye pod that held the taillights, the tips of the wings arched toward each other in a V—the center of which was marked by the Chevy emblem. The license plate sat between the taillights, directly beneath the intersecting point of the wings.

There's no disputing the 1959 El Camino's dramatic appearance, but there's some question that such a wild-looking truck was also designed to work. True, it had a nearly full-sized box that measured 6 1/4ft long and 5 1/4ft wide, with a side height of 12 3/4in, offering a cargo capacity of approximately 32 1/2cu-ft. The problem wasn't space, but capacity. These first El Caminos carried a maximum load rating of 1200lb—just over half a ton—but cargoes of this weight could only be carried by El Caminos that had been fitted with oversized 8.5x14 tires and optional 1530lb-capacity rear springs. Another obstacle to the El Cam-ino's practical use as a pickup was that though the box had quite a generous width, the tailgate measured slightly less than 4 full feet,

Is it a car, or is it a truck? That's the question most people asked when they first saw the new 1959 El Camino pickup in their Chevrolet dealer's showroom. Although the El Camino's dramatic appearance arose from its car origins, nonetheless, this car-pickup was also built to work. Styling aside, the El Camino's most striking feature was the long list of engine options, which included Chevy's fire-breathing 290hp fuel-injected V-8.

making it difficult to load standard 4ft-wide building materials.

Chevrolet offered the 1959 El Camino in two models: the six-cylinder 1180 and the V-8–powered 1280. Buyers of the 1180 model found a shorter option list that omitted air conditioning and some of the transmission choices. On the plus side, an El Camino equipped with Chevrolet's 235ci stovebolt six, now rated at 135hp, offered reliable and economical transportation. The V-8 version had something never seen before in a light truck: a range of engine choices with horsepower ratings well in excess of anything needed to haul a load of 2x4s home from the lumberyard. Model 1280 El Caminos could be special ordered with Chevrolet's hottest engines, including the 290hp fuel-injected 283 mouse motor V-8 and the triple-deuce –carbureted 348 big-block V-8 rated at 335hp. In towns all across America, El Caminos equipped with these hot engine packages burned rubber all the way down Main Street on Friday nights.

Besides the column shift three-speed transmission, gearbox options included a three-speed plus overdrive for those looking for economy, the Corvette four-speed for performance, the unexciting Power-glide for reliability, and the new Turboglide automatic for glassy smooth shifts.

Because of its classification as a truck, the El Camino didn't fall under any of Chevrolet's three model series: Biscayne, Bel Air, or Impala. Externally, however, the car-pickup looked like a Bel Air since it wore the intermediate model line's trim— minus the Bel Air emblems. Inside, all El Caminos carried no-frills Biscayne series upholstery and interior appointments. The standard two-toned gray vinyl seat covering wouldn't show soil from the driver's sliding onto it in dirty work clothes, and the door panels were color matched to the seats; a green or blue interior was sometimes found instead of gray, in combination with a green or blue exterior. Such a drab cab didn't do much for impressing anyone who expected a truck that looked like a car to have more upscale interior. Again, with work in mind, Chevrolet provided the El Camino with a plain rubber mat that could be easily swept clean. The omission of features that had come to be expected in a car, such as dual sun visors and armrests, foam padding on the seat-back and seat bottom, and a padded dash, also showed GM's judgment that though it looked like a car, the El Camino was really a truck. However, the passenger's-side sun visor and armrest, foam padding, and a padded dash could all be added at extra cost.

For 1960 the El Camino received the car line's facelift that softened the 1959 styling features. The choice as to whether Chevrolet's 1959 or 1960 styling is more desirable is really personal preference. The outrageous or glamorous—you decide which—look of 1959 is gaining popularity, but the more subdued 1960 styling has always looked good. As had been Chevrolet's intent from the start, the greatest ap-

peal of these early car-pickups is their potential as "muscle" trucks. Find a 1959 or 1960 with a high-performance engine, and you'll have an exciting truck that will catch the eyes of passersby, whether on the highway, in town, or at shows.

1964-1976 El Caminos

The El Camino disappeared after 1960, largely because of poor sales but also because Ford had downsized the Ranchero to its compact Falcon line and Chevrolet had no suitable platform on which to follow suit with the El Camino— the rear-engined Corvair made designing a standard pickup difficult and a car-based pickup impossible. So the El Camino's revival waited for 1964 and the introduction of the all-new Chevelle midsized car line. The Chevelle platform seemed tailor-made for bringing back Chevrolet's car-pickup. It included a two-door station wagon, which needed only to have the top and window area removed behind the front seat to become a pickup, and, more important, the Chevelle fabrication used a full frame—unlike the unit construction of the somewhat smaller Chevy II. Also important, Chevrolet had decided to give the Chevelle line its full range of engine options. This meant that El Camino buyers could load their trucks with the hottest engines in town— even the 360hp fuel-injected Corvette V-8.

Chevrolet's sales brochures described the new, downsized El Camino as a "personal pickup."

In the sixties Ford was calling its four-seater Thunderbird a "personal car" and Chrysler did the same for its firecracker-hot 300. A personal car was something you drove to enjoy, as opposed to something you used to cart the family to a hamburger joint or to grandma's, or to run back and forth to work. Apparently Chevrolet's marketing people thought the El Camino could enjoy a similar status among pickups—and it has. Although some El Caminos were used for light hauling, most have served the role described in the brochures—as personal transportation to go from here to there for whatever reason.

Part of the downsized El Camino's sales success resulted from letting buyers "build" the El Camino they wanted by selecting an appearance and interior level and picking the engine-drivetrain combination separately. The standard El Camino came with a brightmetal grille, bumpers, and hubcaps, as on the 300 basic model

By the seventies the El Camino's styling began to take on a bloated look. The hood length now equaled or surpassed the cargo area, giving an image of power that no longer existed owing to constrictions in engine performance. However, El Caminos of this styling series have at least one redeeming feature: they exude an image of luxury and comfort unmatched by that of any other truck of the era. Chevrolet Division, General Motors Corporation

Chevelle cars, with vinyl-trimmed seat and door panels in three color schemes, and a color-keyed steering wheel and rubber floor mat. This interior was plush for a

Even though Chevrolet abandoned its Malibu car platform, on which the final series El Camino was based, in 1983, the El Camino remained in production through 1987. An impressive sight to El Camino admirers is the service truck line-up parked in front of this replacement window company in Lancaster, Pennsylvania. One wonders what this company will do for service trucks when its El Caminos finally wear out.

Despite the rakish exterior and sports car engine options, Chevrolet intended the El Camino as a working truck. This particular truck has nonstock Impala upholstery, but if you looked inside a completely stock 1959 model, you would see no-frills Biscayne series interior appointments and gray vinyl seat coverings. Doug Stapleton of Brandenton, Florida, owns this truck.

truck, and the colors were a big improvement over the drab gray of the first El Caminos. The upscale custom El Camino added decorative trim around the wheel cutouts and brightmetal moldings along the bottoms of the rocker panels. Inside, seats covered in vinyl-trimmed nylon cloth, pile carpeting, and a fancier steering

wheel helped carry the personal pickup image. Leather-grained bucket seats could be optioned at extra cost.

Chevrolet carried the 1964 Chevelle body stampings for four years, but a new grille, with cutouts into the front fenders, gave the 1966 and 1967 models a less blunted frontal look, which improved the

overall styling substantially. In 1966 Chevrolet introduced the Chevelle SS styling package, which included a blacked-out grille, fake hood scoops, and crossed racing flags over the SS emblem attached to the front fenders. The SS also became an El Camino option and included the high-performance 396ci V-8. Available in 325hp or 360hp ratings, the 396 engine was a pavement scorcher and altered the El Camino's image from that of a smartly styled personal pickup to that of a rumble-exhaust muscle truck. A new grille, with larger slots, and other changes to the front end detail set apart the 1967 models. Wraparound taillights that could be seen from the side of the truck were another way to spot a 1967 El Camino.

Along with the rest of the Chevelle line, the El Camino received all-new styling in 1968. Notable changes included a 5 1/2in increase in overall length, sloping rooflines at the sides of the cab that lent a more streamlined look, and more rounded contours on both the sides and the rear of

the truck. Nearly the entire wheelbase stretch occurred ahead of the box, so the cargo dimensions remained the same as on the previous models. The new styling looked good. Cab height increased by 3in, but the increased use of curved and flowing lines camouflaged the taller profile.

With annual front end facelifts, the 1968 styling remained in production through 1972. Although probably every El Camino fancier has her or his favorite, the year most often voted all-time best-looking is 1970 and the model wearing the beauty crown is that year's El Camino SS. A brief review of the styling evolution seen on Chevelle models between 1968 and 1972 will show why.

For 1968, the El Camino—and Chevy's Chevelle car line—carried a grille that looked right out of 1966, except for hoods over the headlights and the grille's side indent running all the way down to the bottom of the front fenders. No major disturbance of this look occurred in 1969. To recognize a 1969, look for a bar across

the middle of the grille, with the Chevrolet bow-tie emblem in the center. Stylists waited until the 1970 models to exercise their creativity. The new frontal design gave a taller grille opening that the SS model accentuated with wide racing stripes running down the center of the hood. The reason El Camino connoisseurs prefer the 1970 frontal styling to that of 1971 and 1972 is the 1970's quieter, painted grille as opposed to the "tinsel"-decked grilles of the 1971 and 1972 models. The painted headlight housings of the 1970 design also gave a more subdued look than the successor models' bright-metal headlight surrounds and more prominent parking lights, mounted on the leading edges of the front fenders. Natu-

This 1959 El Camino's original buyer had hauling at the drag races in mind. Hot Rod magazine ran a 90mph standing-start quarter-mile and turned 0-60mph times of 8.7 seconds with a similarly equipped 348 big-block El Camino.

rally, styling is 99 percent personal preference and not one truck in Chevy's 1968-72 stable, be it El Camino or pickup, wouldn't look great poking out of anyone's garage.

"Carlike luxury—El Camino toughness." That's how the sales brochure described the 1970 models. Even with stan-

The most stunning of all El Caminos are the limited number of designer series models specially modified by Choo Choo Customs. These vehicles, which were built in low numbers from 1983 to 1987, are easily recognized by their unique National Association of Stock Car Auto Racing-style (NASCAR) aerodynamic front end. This example is owned by Jean Allan. Courtesy Jean Allan

dard interior furnishings, the new El Camino series fit the luxury description for a light truck. The base interior now included carpeting and color-keyed vinyl door and seat coverings available in saddle, blue, and black. Moving up, the Custom interior offered deep textured vinyl seat coverings, wood-grained trim on the instrument panel, and added color options. The SS 396 package brought a sporting

flair to the truck's interior with bucket seats, full gauges that included a tachometer, and an optional center console. Accessories ran practically the whole gamut of dress-up and convenience options found in the Chevelle car line, plus some unique truck items.

El Caminos ordered with the SS 396 package also came equipped with front disc brakes, sport wheels, heavy-duty

Due to the absence of a two-door station wagon in its 1961 passenger car line, Chevrolet discontinued its stylish El Camino pickup after 1960. The car-pickup resumed with its introduction of the Chevelle midsized line in 1964. The Chevelle's styling and size fit the El Camino to a T and sales soared. The '65 El Camino seen here is owned by Bill Worthington of Apopka, Florida. It is powered by the L79 350hp 327 engine. In the background is a 1965 Chevelle SS convertible owned by Charles Stinson of Mt. Dora, Florida.

In a collector's eyes, spinner hubcaps like this one on a 1965 model are a highly desirable accessory.

Marketed as a personal pickup, the Chevelle-based El Camino featured more colorful interiors and greater comfort. The example seen here is a 1965 Custom model.

When loaded down with air conditioning and power accessories, the small-block V-8 pretty well filled this 1965 El Camino's engine compartment. (The air cleaner decal and intake manifold are not correct for this L79 327.)

springs, stabilizer bars, a different instrument panel, and special hood, plus the SS trim and hood stripes in some years. To boost load capacity, the car-pickups could also be fitted with air booster shocks, which were inflated through an air valve that mounted on the parcel shelf above the spare tire, just behind the passenger's seat.

Through the late sixties and into the early seventies, GM counted the El Camino among its "muscle car" offerings. For 1967 performance buyers could

choose between a 327ci V-8 rated at either 275hp or 325hp, and the big-block 396 in either 325hp or 350hp form. As a pickup, the El Camino was not a particularly heavy vehicle, and powering one of these runabouts with a 350hp engine was like tying a JATO bottle to a skateboard. For the restyled 1968 El Camino, engine ratings stayed the same, but the new 400lb heavier body reduced performance slightly. To overcome the extra weight, Chevy replaced the 327 in 1969, with its new 350ci small-block V-8, and boosted the output of the big-block 396 to 375hp. For 1970 a 454ci big-block engine, rated at either 360hp or 450hp, could be ordered. Standing on the "go" pedal of a 450hp El Camino could shred the rear tires to the carcass as easily as saying, "See the

Next page
A highly collectible 1970 El Camino SS 396. Counterbalancing the bold hood stripes, the SS package included more subdued painted headlight housings and a general absence of "tinsel." Carl Beck of Clearwater, Florida, owns this El Camino.

USA in your Chevrolet... ." This was the high-water mark of El Camino performance. In 1971, owing to increasingly stringent clean air regulations, the top power rating of the 454 backed off to 425hp, and within a few years, the big power ratings on Chevy's big V-8s had fallen to those of a healthy six in 1970.

If you're a muscle car admirer and wondering, "why not a pickup?" you

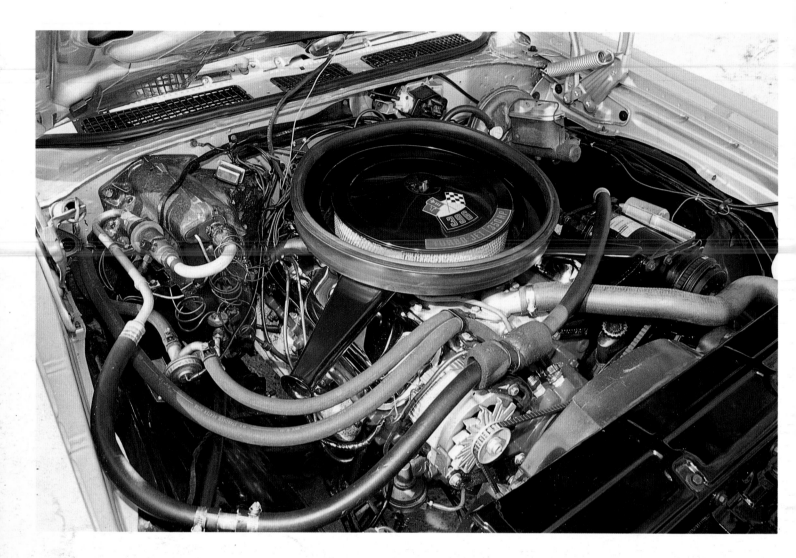

Now here's a sight that will send a mechanic running out for his coffee break! By 1970, the typical V-8 engine compartment was a hopeless maze of hoses and wires. This engine is from a 1970 El Camino SS 396.

should seriously consider tracking down one of the very limited number of legitimate high-performance El Caminos. But don't make the purchase until you're sure the engine is legitimate. As with performance cars, the value of a muscle truck is directly tied to whether the engine is original to the truck. This means you have to make sure the truck's engine hasn't been recycled from a wreck. Let's say, for example, you buy a 1970 El with a big-block 454, but the data plate shows that this truck originally carried a 230 six. This truck's value will be that of the base six-cylinder, minus a few percentage points for the wrong engine. No way should that truck sell in the muscle price range. But if

the 454 shows on the data plate, it's the same as having a pedigree or being born into aristocracy: everything's kosher, and the hefty muscle car premium applies. Data plate decoding information can be found in the book *Catalog of Chevrolet Truck ID Numbers, 1946-1972*.

If your checkbook doesn't say yes to a Ferrari Testa Rossa, you can still feel the punch of an F-14 with a muscle El Camino at a price to which your banker might say yes.

In keeping with American car builders' belief that bigger is better, Chevy's third Chevelle-based El Camino series, introduced in 1973, swelled 12in in overall length and 1in in width. A 2in decrease in overall height added a visual impression of even greater length. Since the wheelbase remained the same at 116in, the longer styling resulted in extending the front and rear overhangs, not an especially desirable feature on a truck. The rear wheels on this series El Camino sat almost under the front

of the box, making the cargo area look almost like an afterthought.

As bloated as these mid-seventies cars—and car-pickups—look today, the auto makers may have had their finger on the public's pulse when the cars were new. The restyled El Camino was a resounding sales success, with 72,000 El Caminos and Sprints combined being produced in 1975. But the El Camino had reached the crest of its popularity. The oil embargo, coming at the start of the next model year, quickly soured Americans on fuel-ravenous, overstuffed cars—or in this case, car-pickups. The lack of an economy engine—the six had been dropped in 1973—further hurt El Camino sales as motorists saw gasoline prices jump from 30 to 50 cents a gallon, then climb to near the dollar-a-gallon mark. Adding insult to injury, the performance of the El Camino's big-displacement V-8s—the 307 engine was now standard—had fallen to near or below that of the standard six of a few

years previously. For 1973 the base 307 engine had a rating of just 115hp. Even the beefy 454 now mustered only a modest 245hp, and its fuel economy was atrocious.

To promote the 1974 El Camino, Chevrolet ad writers coined the slogan, "So Comfortable, You're Surprised It's So Practical." Let's compare this slogan, so appropriate for this third midsized El Camino styling series, with the slogans of the previous two series. The first Chevelle-based El Camino had been called a personal pickup. Then, in the second styling series, the emphasis shifted to luxury. Now the ad writers were stressing comfort—and for good reason. The new seat coverings of leather-like vinyl or a combination of cloth and vinyl, did indeed make for riding comfort. A somewhat novel interior feature—bucket seats that swung around a full 90 degrees,

so that all you had to do to exit the truck was step down onto the pavement—further enhanced the comfort image.

1978-1987 El Caminos

For 1978 Chevrolet dropped the Chevelle name and used the Malibu nameplate—which formerly had identified the deluxe Chevelle models—on its midsized cars. Although the El Camino resembled the Malibu car line from a styling and engineering standpoint, it did not wear Malibu badges.

When seen alongside its 1973-77 predecessors, the 1978 El Camino appeared to have undergone a crash diet, yet little was lost in interior or cargo space. A reduction of 12in in overall length eliminated some of the previous model's overhang, and designers compensated for the new styling's narrower width by slimming

Rich, leather-look bucket seats gave this 1970 El Camino SS the feel and appearance of an expensive sports car.

the door profiles. Side quarter windows and a reverse-curved rear window allowed for greater glass area.

Early years in this final El Camino series were easy to distinguish by changes to the grille. For 1978 the Malibu-based El Camino sported a lattice-style grille flanked by single headlights and parking lights set in the leading edge of the front fenders, where they doubled as marker lights. For 1979 the grille consisted of four narrow rectangles, stacked one on top of the other, with a center divider. The headlight and parking light treatment remained unchanged. For 1980 the grille retained its rectangular shape but now featured narrow vertical dividers. In 1981 the dividers aligned horizontally. From 1982 to the end in 1987, frontal styling remained unchanged. The final grille design took on the egg-crate shape that always seems to look right on a Chevrolet. Quad headlights set over smaller, rectangular sets of parking-signal lights carried the grille's crosshatch motif across the front of the truck.

For this last styling series, Chevrolet offered the El Camino in three special trim packages: the Royal Knight, Conquista, and Super Sport. The Royal Knight was easily recognized by a massive coat of arms–style hood decal, similar to the Firebird decal applied to the hood of Pontiac's Trans Am sport coupe. This trim package positioned the El Camino as a sporty sedan-pickup for younger buyers. Targeted past the youth set, the Conquista offered tasteful two-toned exterior color schemes, bright side moldings, dress-up wheel covers, and luxurious, color-keyed interiors. Conquistas could most easily be recognized by the identifying decal on the tailgate. The Super Sport served as the El Camino's deluxe model. It featured a large front air dam, decal accent stripes, rally wheels, Super Sport identification on the lower doors, and dual sport mirrors.

In addition to Chevrolet's special El Camino models, Choo Choo Customs of Chattanooga, Tennessee, built a number of special designer series El Caminos, beginning in 1983 and continuing through 1987, that carried numerous custom features. A Choo Choo Customs El Camino was easily recognized by its unique aerodynamic front end, machine-turned aluminum side moldings, two-toned dark blue-and-white paint scheme, and special designer series door handles. Although Choo Choo Customs will not release the production total, only a modest number were built. In 1994, the Choo Choo Customs Designer Series El Camino held the price record for collectible vintage trucks.

Although Chevrolet phased out the Malibu line in 1983, replacing it with the front-drive Celebrity series, the El Camino continued in production for five more years. When Chevrolet finally dropped the El Camino, it did so with no fanfare; the last car-pickup just faded away. Besides the expense of tooling for a new model, GM no doubt reasoned that the new-generation C-1500 trucks with their carlike luxury and handling filled the role once served by a car-based pickup.

Any El Camino is an appealing truck. An advantage of this last series is that well-cared-for examples are still to be found—particularly those built toward the end of the run. Like the last of any series, these handsome trucks should appreciate in value.

The GMC Sprint

The El Camino remained an exclusively Chevrolet product until 1971. In that year GMC introduced its El Camino variant called the Sprint. This car-pickup differed from its Chevrolet twin only in the Sprint and GMC nameplates. Mechanically, and in overall styling, the Sprint and the El Camino were the same vehicle. From a collector standpoint, Sprints are considerably rarer, though this doesn't necessarily make them more valuable, since the El Camino nameplate has greater familiarity and therefore generates more interest.

In 1978 when the El Camino took on Chevrolet's midsized Malibu styling, GMC changed the name of its El Camino clone to Caballero. Someone at GMC apparently liked Spanish names, because the upgrade trim packages offered on the Caballero were called Diablo, Laredo, and Amarillo. The Diablo package came with a hood-sized decal depicting a stylized devil and flames, as well as the Diablo identification in large outline letters on the doors, dual sport mirrors, and rally wheels. The Laredo, offered earlier in the run, and the Amarillo, the same model with a different name in a later run, approximated Chevrolet's El Camino Super Sport in trim and options.

Caballero interiors and engine options matched those of the Chevrolet El Camino, with the diesel also being offered in the 1983 and 1984 models. GMC also built the Caballero through 1987. Find one of these trucks, and you're not likely to see another like it for a long time.

To most truck fanciers, the El Camino hit its high water mark, both in styling and performance, with the 1977 SS model seen here. El Caminos of the 1968 to 72 styling series are slightly larger than their Chevelle-based predecessors, yet are free of the bloated, misproportioned look of the 1973-77 models. After 1970, federal laws designed to limit engine emissions led to a decrease in performance and a drastic decline in fuel economy—added reasons for selecting a 1970 or earlier El Camino as a collector vehicle.

Chapter 13

Corvair 95, 1961-1965

Chevrolet referred to its compact commercial models built on the Corvair platform simply as Model 95s—a number representing the wheelbase measurement of 95in—and placed them in the 1200 series. Body types consisted of two pickups, the side-door-loading Rampside and the standard tailgate-style Loadside; the cargo-carrying Corvan; and the passenger-carrying Greenbrier van. None of the Corvair commercial models caught the public's fancy. The Greenbrier passenger van had the longest production run, 1961-65, and highest sales, 57,986 units total. The Loadside pickup survived only two years, 1961 and 1962, and sold only 2,844 copies. The more practical Rampside fared better, with production extending through 1964 and sales reaching 17,786 units. The Corvan and the Greenbrier shared the odd fate of competing against their more orthodox front-engined successor: The Chevy II-–based front-engined Chevy van put the Corvan out of production in 1964 after a

Unlike the compact pickups from Ford and Dodge, Chevrolet's small Corvair-based trucks represented a fresh look at pickup design. Since the air-cooled rear engine created an uneven load floor, Chevrolet engineers built a load door into the passenger side of the pickup box. The idea was that long items could be loaded in from the pickup's rear, while heavy, bulky items could be wheeled into the forward section of the pickup box.

Owing to their many innovative features, Model 95 pickups are a collector favorite, particularly the Rampside model with its unique side door that lowers to form a loading ramp. Jean Allan, who owns this Model 95 example, staged this humorous pose that suggests a tiny Crosley "roundside" pickup could be driven onto her Corvair Rampside by the loading ramp door.

dismal Corvan run of only 8,147 units. The Greenbrier fielded a 1965 model but saw only 1,528 built.

Chevrolet's Corvair-based commercial models were far better vehicles than their sales figures suggest. A number of Corvair experts agree that it wasn't the Model 95's unorthodox engineering that turned buyers off—it was price. GM had high tooling costs to amortize, and low-volume sales meant a higher per-unit bite for the expense of getting the Corvair cars and commercials into production. So, though

those in the market for a downsized pickup or van might look hard and long at a Model 95, chances are they would buy up (or down) the street at the Ford dealer, where the new Econoline compacts with their traditional front engine and Falcon underpinnings could undercut a Model 95 even on the salesperson's first price quote. But as Corvair cars and Model 95 commercials got out into the public, another sales stigma developed: Chevrolet's early compacts had problems big time. The engines leaked so much oil that the heaters were known to duct blue smoke into the vehicle. Also, the transaxle hinged the rear wheels the same way as on a Volkswagen (VW), so if one wheel actually got airborne, it could tuck under like an aircraft landing gear. Then, when the wheel came back down, only the outer tire edge made contact with the pavement. When this happened, the vehicle usually flipped over—leading consumer advocate Ralph Nader to declare GM's Corvair and its pickup and van offshoots to be "unsafe at any speed."

The independent rear suspension that so scared Nader also had a plus side. It gave Chevrolet's Corvair-based Model 95s a handling sophistication and a degree of riding comfort equaled by those of no other American-built pickup or van. Although a little risky in the hands of an unskilled driver, Corvair commercials were a delight to drive. At the time I was driving Corvair

As can be seen in this comparison of a Dodge and a Chevrolet Model 95, the Corvair-based pickup represented a number of revolutionary features—including cab-forward styling, which gave the driver unsurpassed forward visibility and a rear engine for excellent traction. Anyone who has driven one of GM's first compact pickups probably agrees that these were much better trucks than their sluggish sales figures suggest.

vans and Greenbriers, I also owned a Porsche 356 Super 90 coupe and a 1961 Corvette. The handling and driving qualities of the Corvair commercials came close to matching those of the Porsche, and its cornering abilities far exceeded those of the Corvette.

One of the most striking features of any Model 95 was its low height. Trucks of the sixties stood tall, but not Chevy's Corvair-based compacts. Yet the low height didn't crimp inside headroom. And the cab-forward design that put the windshield nearly at the front of the vehicle gave unbeatable forward vision. Sure, the first time you drive a Model 95, you feel as though you are sitting on the front bumper—we've gotten comfortable thinking all that iron under the hood will protect us in a frontal collision—but a few miles down the road, and the seating position will seem as natural as bare feet on a sandy beach.

Although Chevrolet's engineers had undoubtedly looked long and hard at the VW, the Corvair was anything but a VW clone. Of course, there were similarities—on both, the engine was rear mounted, used a pancake layout, and was air cooled, and both featured four-wheel independent suspension—but look at the differences. The Corvair engine had six-cylin-

ders, the VW four; Corvair used a coil spring suspension, VW torsion bars. In other features the Corvair-based Model 95 commercials were unique. Rather than mount the load platform above the engine, which was VW's solution to constructing a pickup on a rear engine chassis, Model 95 pickups had a stepped floor, with the raised portion covering the engine and a sunken section behind the cab. Here's how the bi-level pickup box worked: If you were carrying long, flat cargo, like building materials, you could put a false floor over the sunken box area and just slide in the load. But if you were carrying smaller, bulkier cargo, like a refrigerator or some other household appliance, the load could sit in the front section, where it was protected by the higher box sides and kept from sliding back in the box by the raised rear section. For loading ease Chevrolet designed a unique pickup, called the Rampside, that had a swing-down door cut into the passenger's side of the body. As the name implied, this side door also served as a ramp for loading cargo. Model 95 Rampside pickups were especially handy for carrying wheeled implements, like lawn mowers, that could simply be driven or pushed up the ramp and into the pickup body. To prevent the side door from becoming marred or scratched when it was lowered for loading, the door's top edge was protected with a rubber pad.

Chevrolet never intended its Model 95s as head-on competition with VWs. Besides offering a larger, more powerful engine, an optional automatic transmission, and far better styling, Chevrolet also packed its rear-engined vans and pickups with thoughtful features that wouldn't have existed had economy been the bot-

tom line. For example, double-walled cargo doors on the van models prevented sliding cargo from marring the vehicle's outside appearance. On Greenbrier passenger vans, standard roll-up–roll-down rear windows flooded the interior with fresh air for riding comfort even in a heat wave. Chevy aimed its Corvair-based commercial line at an up-class economy market.

The Greenbrier passenger van was a perfect example of the Model 95's upscale position in the hot new van market. Besides attractive exterior paint schemes that added a contrasting color to the waistline and posh-for-the-period interiors, Chevrolet gave the Greenbrier a long list of accessories that included camping gear that transformed the space-efficient van into a "camper extraordinaire." Everything but the kitchen sink—that's almost literally what the camper package included. When it was fully set up, a camper family could prepare meals from food kept fresh in an onboard refrigerator and cooked on a gas stove, eat on a table that mounted between the middle seats, sleep on beds made by placing special cushions over the seats, enjoy bug-free comfort thanks to window screens, relish the convenience of a port-a-potty, and keep warm with a gas-fired heater. Records show the camper to have attracted only 300 buyers. Three existed in 1994—making this a very rare Chevrolet light commercial model.

Corvair and Model 95 owners and collectors are a proud bunch—and rightfully so. Their organization—CORSA, short for the Corvair Society of America—is thoroughly convinced that Chevy's first compacts got a bum rap from the consumer movement and deserved better than GM's quiet abandonment. Besides holding

shows to display Corvair cars and Model 95s, CORSA also has regional chapters and publishes a newsletter packed with historical information and technical tips. Thanks to modern sealants, CORSA's technical experts have even licked the flat-six Corvair engine's notorious oil leak problem.

There's no question that Chevrolet Model 95s carried the smartest-looking small truck styling of their day. GM could dust off these trucks today, replace the quad headlights with modern rectangular halogen units, fit flush-mounted glass, and black out the chrome, and the snub-nosed pickups and vans would look hot off the stylists' sketchpads. Of course, the rear en-

gine went out with the VW Beetle, so to bring a Model 95 into the nineties, it would need a transverse front engine. But all this is dreaming. Chevy's Corvair-based commercials represented a big leap in engineering and design, that was lost on consumers who looked only at the bottom line. But collectors aren't in the same position, and owning a Model 95, whether a Rampside or Loadside pickup, a cargo van, or a Greenbrier passenger van, is to experience sixties ingenuity at its best.

Model 95s have a couple of other pluses from a collector standpoint. They're a styling league apart from everything else, so they capture plenty of attention—

To make loading heavy, bulky items as easy as pushing a grocery cart, the Rampside's load door hinged at the bottom, allowing it to swing down onto the ground, where it could serve as a ramp. Despite the practical benefits of this novel load door arrangement, the public had difficulty accepting the Corvair pickup's unorthodox design. Francis Lux of Ladson, South Carolina, owns this beautiful 1961 Rampside.

whether at shows or running up the highway—and they're a driver's delight. Just don't whale a Corvair commercial (or pre-1965 Corvair car) hard on the corners.

Although light-duty trucks are far more popular with collectors than big trucks, the unique styling of the heavy-duty COE models built by Chevy from the late thirties through the end of the Advance Design series in 1955, has a special appeal that is capturing collector interest.

Perhaps the cutest pickup you'll ever see: Ric Hall built this shorty snub-nose using the cab from a two-ton Advance Design series COE truck.

Ric Hall's COE pickup almost looks like something Chevy might have built. Wonder why they didn't?

Chapter 14

COE—Cab-Over-Engine—Trucks, 1939-1955

From the late thirties through the fifties, the Big Three US truck builders—Chevy, Ford, and Dodge—marketed distinctive-looking snub-nosed models known as COEs, Cab-Over-Engines. The advantage of the COE design was greater cargo area for a given wheelbase. Not only were COEs more maneuverable, their high cab perch also gave drivers excellent forward visibility—a real plus when threading a truck through traffic. Besides leaving its imprint on today's road haulers, most of which have adopted the flat-nosed design, the benefit of added cargo space on a short wheelbase led to the use of COE styling for the compact pickups that appeared in the late fifties and early sixties—notably the VW Transporter, Willys Forward Control, Corvair Rampside and Loadside pickups, Ford Econoline pickup, and imitative Dodge A-100 pickup.

A special breed of collectors really take to COE model trucks. Fitted with a late-model engine and either a two-speed or a modern rear axle, they make great haulers for that vintage light truck or car. Besides, they're unusual. COEs weren't strong sellers when new—most buyers seemed to prefer the standard long-nosed jobs—and today a whole generation hasn't seen a vintage COE truck. Through each styling change, the COEs kept a strong family resemblance with their long-nosed cousins by a shared cab—with different doors that contained cutouts for the wheel arch—

and similar grille designs. Although the most popular Chevrolet light trucks are the late-forties, early-fifties Advance Design models, COE admirers prefer their trucks to have the tall grille design found on the late-thirties and early-forties models.

Chevrolet introduced its COE model trucks in 1939. Early in World War II, Chevy built a few COEs with a front drive axle—most of which went to the military. These trucks are extremely rare, and it is not known if any have survived. Production figures of COE trucks are unclear, but during the Advance Design era, about 1,000 were made each year. In 1956 Chevy replaced the COE with a lower-profile, short-nosed design called the Low Cab Forward (LCF).

Generally called two-ton trucks, Chevrolet's COEs were rated at up to 15,000lb GVW and ran the tried-and-true 216ci and 235ci stovebolt Chevy six engines plus four-speed transmission, with a two-speed rear axle optional at extra cost.

Shorty Snub-nose

Thinking that if COE-style big trucks looked good, a COE pickup ought to look even better, Ric Hall, a Sumner, Washington, truck enthusiast, set out to build a stunningly cute tall-cab street rod pickup.

Starting with the cab and chassis from a two-ton Advance Design series Chevrolet COE truck, Hall's first step—after removing the cab—was to cut out the cab's

single-window rear section and replace it with a three-window rear section from a deluxe cab; the front of the COE cab was slightly different to clear the wheelwells, so Hall found it easier to take a rear corner panel section from a pickup cab than to locate a deluxe COE cab. To keep his truck looking "period," Hall chose a short pickup box from a 1954 Chevy half-ton pickup, which he dressed up with a very rare 1954 Chevy pickup chrome rear bumper. This bumper had a stamped-in center dip that made it unique to that year.

The underpinnings of Hall's shorty COE consisted of a 1973 Chevy pickup rear frame section sandwiched into the front frame rails from the two-ton COE. Rather than using the big truck's front suspension and steering, Hall fitted the 1973 pickup's front cross-member and coil spring suspension into the big truck's forward frame section. Incredibly, the COE's front frame width matched that of the 1973 pickup, allowing the pickup's front cross-member to bolt in place. The wheelbase worked out to 91in with only a 16in drive shaft tying a Turbo Hydra-matic 400 transmission and 1971 Cadillac 472ci engine to the 1973 Chevy half-ton rear end.

Hall stated that his shorty COE turns heads everywhere it goes—and that it's a sure trophy winner at shows. The neatest thing about Hall's shorty snub-nose is that the truck looks like something Chevy might have built. Wonder why it didn't?

Buyers of late-model Chevrolet trucks had the 5.0L (shown here) and 5.7L V-8 engine among their engine options. The 5.0L model was more common on trucks used for general transportation while the 5.7L engine was more common in work trucks purchased for hauling and towing.

Chevrolet Division, General Motors Corporation

Chapter 15

Engines

Stovebolt. That's the nickname given to the overhead valve six-cylinder engine shared by all Chevrolet cars and light trucks built between 1929 and 1955. The nickname wasn't a putdown, but picked up on the engine's simplicity, which some have compared with that of a Briggs and Stratton lawn mower engine. Although the stovebolt's basic design stretched from 1929 to 1962, the engine went through several upgrades over this thirty-three-year period.

The original Chevy six, as it appeared in 1929, featured three main bearings, displaced 194ci, and put out 50hp at 2800 rpm. By putting a six in its lowest-price car, GM handily one-upped Ford, its arch competitor, which would continue to offer only an L-head four into mid-1932. In its earliest version, the stovebolt six inhaled its fuel mixture through an updraft carburetor. For 1932 the carburetor arrangement became downdraft and power output increased to 53hp on trucks, 60hp on Chevy cars. The engine's next change occurred in 1933 when the stroke increased to 4in, from 3.75in. This increased displacement to 206.8ci, and horsepower rose to 65hp at 3000rpm.

In 1937 the stovebolt six underwent its first major redesign—a reworking so thorough that few parts interchanged from previous production. Actually, about the only similarity between this engine and the 1929-36 Chevy six was the loca-

tion of the engine number, which continued to be stamped on the side of the block next to the fuel pump. For greater durability, the crankshaft now turned on four main bearings. However, no changes were made to the low-pressure oiling system and poured Babbitt bearings. By increasing the cylinder bore to 4in, while returning the stroke to the original 3.75in, the

The stovebolt six engine found in Chevy trucks from 1929 to 1963 had the reliability and nearly the simplicity of a Briggs and Stratton lawn mower engine.

engineers stretched the engine's displacement to 216.5ci. Quite surprisingly, this larger engine actually had a 2in-shorter

This 1993 version of the V-6 truck engine was found in many late-model Chevrolet pickups. This 4.3L EFI Vortec V-6 had a displacement of 262ci and produced 165hp at 4000rpm. Chevrolet Division, General Motors Corporation

block. The 216, as this engine came to be called, would remain in production in trucks through 1953.

A new, still larger version of the stovebolt six joined Chevrolet's engine line-up in 1941. This powerplant, which displaced 235ci, initially saw service in the company's medium-duty truck models, and did not become available in light trucks until 1954. Externally, the early 235s and the 216 looked identical. Owing to the ease with which 235 and 216 engines interchanged, it's not at all unusual to find that the original 216 in an Art Deco or Advance Design Chevy pickup has been replaced by a 235 from a bigger truck or newer car or pickup. A fairly significant change occurred in 1948 when both engines adopted interchangeable replaceable thin-walled connecting rod bearings. However, on both engines the main bearings remained the poured Babbitt type and lubrication continued to be supplied by a low-pressure oil system.

On pickups the long-overdue upgrade to replaceable main bearings and full-pressure oiling finally arrived in 1954, with the adoption of Chevy's Powerglide 235 into the light-truck line. This engine continued to be supplied in Chevrolet cars and light trucks, largely unchanged, through 1962. The final stovebolt offshoot, a 261ci version, appeared the same year in the medium- and heavier-duty trucks. This "macho" engine also sometimes appeared in earlier Chevy pickups.

Six-cylinder Truck Engine Casting Numbers

Year	Description	Block Number	Head Number
1929	All	835501	835503
1930	All	836409	
1930-31	All	836273, 836275	
1932	All	836573	936718
1933-34	CA, DA Master and truck	837231	836961, 837230
1935-36	All	836010	837981
1937-38	All	838710	838355
1937-40	All		838773
1939	All	838941	
1940	All	839132	
1941	216 passenger and truck	839400	
	235 truck	3660439	
1941-48	All 216, 235	839401	
1942-47	216 passenger and truck	839770	839910
	235 truck	3835335	839751
1948-49	216 passenger and truck	3835253	
	235 truck	3835309	
1949	All 216, 235	3835409	
1950-51	216 passenger and truck	3835497	
	235 truck	3692713	
1950-52	235	3835499, 3835909	
1950-53	All 216	3835517	
1952	235 passenger with PG, truck	3835692	
1952-53	216 passenger and truck	3835849	
1953	235, standard transmission	3701946	3701887
1954-55	235, First Series 1955	3701481	3835913
		3835911	
		3733949	
	261, First Series 1955	3702436	3835499
		3703414	3708570
		3733950	3836850
1955-57	235, Second Series 1955	3835911	3836848
	261 truck	3836340	3708570
		3837012	3836850
1958	261, Stellite valves	3788813	3836850
1958-62	235, front side mount	3738307	3835913
		3764476	3836848
1959	261, side mount	3739365	3836850
		3769925	
1960-62	235, front center mount	3738307	3836848
		3739716	
		3764476	
	261, front center mount	3739365	3836850
		3769717	

Although Chevy trucks used only three slightly different versions of the same engine for over three decades, restorers encounter problems trying to identify whether or not their truck's engine is the original. Usually a quick visual inspection will tell whether the truck has the correct *type* of engine; zeroing in on whether or not the engine is likely to be original takes closer scrutiny. The quick way to tell if a pre-1963 six-cylinder–powered Chevy truck has the right engine for its year is to look at the pushrod cover on the engine's right-hand (passenger's) side. All 216s and 235s built before 1950 had a tall pushrod cover that extended from the oil pan all the way up to the spark plug holes. All 235s built in 1950 and later had a short pushrod cover that did not extend to the spark plug holes. The 261 had a slightly taller block, though this difference is not easily recognized. More precise identification of a vintage Chevy pickup's six-cylinder engine can be made by comparing the truck's engine casting number against the following chart.

A "built" Chevy six makes a heady performer and great-sounding engine with split Fenton headers and a multiple-carburetor manifold. Today correct reproductions of these popular "hot rod" accessories are still available from Patrick's (P.O. Box 10648, Casa Grande, AZ 85230). But for real performance, and to out-sprint a Ford V-8, the historic answer has been a GMC six equipped with such speed-up goodies as Fenton headers and a multiple-carburetor Howard intake. The GMC six, first introduced in 1939, shared design parentage with the Chevy stovebolt but featured pressure oiling. Since GMC sixes through 1953 displaced only 228ci, the popular GMC swaps are the 1954-and-later 248 and the 1956-and-later 270.

In 1955 Chevrolet made automotive headlines with its radically different small-block V-8 mouse motor. The original version of this engine, which remains in production today, displaced only 265ci, but its easy-breathing nature—fostered by a superlight valvetrain—made the mouse motor a hot performer from the get-go.

Greatly to their credit, Chevrolet chief engineer Ed Cole and his design team started with a fresh sheet of paper. Instead of installing the complex shaft mechanism for supporting the overhead valve rocker arms, they reduced the pivoting parts to simple stampings that mounted directly to the head by a pressed-in stud. Presto: not only a much simpler, less-costly-to-produce valve mechanism, but also a greatly reduced valvetrain mass. Couple lightness with size, and you have Chevy's enduring small-block V-8. Early mouse motors can be recognized by the absence of a full-flow fuel filter, but in external appearances, the various versions differ little. In 1958 Chevy trucks received the larger 283in engine that had become available in cars in 1957, and in 1966 displacement stepped up to 327ci. For 1968 a downsized, and less muscular, 307 became available, and in 1969 the mouse motor reached its ultimate form—the legendary 350 (5.7-liter) engine that *Car and Driver* magazine has heralded as one of the ten best engine designs of all time.

Clubs

Classic Chevy Cameo and GMC Suburban Pickup Club
4505 S. County Rd. 7
Midland, TX 79073

The Cameo and Suburban Club is a regional organization headquartered in the south. This group publishes a small newsletter and encourages restoration and preservation of 1955-57 Chevy Cameo and GMC Suburban pickups.

Corvair Society of America (CORSA)
P.O. Box 550
Midlothian, IL 60445

Formed by and for those who appreciate the Corvair automobile, CORSA is a national club that publishes a monthly magazine called the CORSA *Communique*. The publication includes feature articles, news and events, technical articles, and classified ads. The club sponsors an annual convention and sanctions various regional events. It also sponsors a museum fund to protect and preserve Corvair memorabilia. The group welcomes owners of Corvair 95 (commercial) vehicles.

Inliners International
R.D. 3, Box 83, Rt. 44
Pleasant Valley, NY 12569

Inliners International is a national club devoted to early Chevy and GMC racing engines and other inliners. The organization publishes a bimonthly newsletter, the *12 Port News*, which contains technical articles, features, and racing news and offers free ad privileges to members. The group sponsors an annual inliners picnic.

Vintage Chevrolet Club of America (VCCA)
P.O. Box 5387
Orange, CA 92613

With over 7,000 members, the VCCA is probably the largest exclusively Chevrolet club. Regions in various areas of the United States sponsor a variety of activities and get-togethers. Members receive a quality monthly publication, which presents articles on Chevrolets from 1912-1975.

Further Reading

Catalog of Chevrolet Truck ID Numbers, 1946-1972, Motorbooks International
Chevrolet Pickups, 1946-1972, Motorbooks International

Heavyweight Book of American Light Duty Trucks, 1939-1966, Motorbooks International

How to Restore Your Chevrolet Pickup, Motorbooks International
Illustrated Chevrolet Pickup Buyer's Guide, Motorbooks International

Index